W9-AZE-794

The Concise Guide to

MS-DOS® 5.0

SPECIAL
EDITION

Microsoft
PRESS

JoAnne Woodcock

PUBLISHED BY
Microsoft Press
A Division of Microsoft Corporation
One Microsoft Way
Redmond, Washington 98052-6399

Library of Congress Cataloging-in-Publication Data

Woodcock, JoAnne.
    The concise guide to MS-DOS 5 / JoAnne Woodcock.
        p.   cm. -- (Microsoft quick reference)
    Includes index.
    ISBN 1-55615-465-8
    1. Operating systems (Computers)   2. MS-DOS (Computer file)
I. Title.   II. Series.
QA76.76.O63W6615   1991
005.4'46--dc20   91-32101
                                                            CIP

Printed and bound in the United States of America.

    2 3 4 5 6 7 8 9   MLML   6 5 4 3 2 1

Distributed to the book trade in Canada by Macmillan of Canada, a division of
Canada Publishing Corporation.

Distributed to the book trade outside the United States and Canada by Penguin
Books Ltd.

Penguin Books Ltd., Harmondsworth, Middlesex, England
Penguin Books Australia Ltd., Ringwood, Victoria, Australia
Penguin Books N.Z. Ltd., 182–190 Wairau Road, Auckland 10, New Zealand

British Cataloging-in-Publication Data available.

As used in this book, DOS refers to the Microsoft MS-DOS operating system and
the IBM version of the MS-DOS operating system, also known as PC-DOS.

Intel® is a registered trademark of Intel Corporation. IBM® is a registered
trademark of International Business Machines Corporation. Microsoft®
and MS-DOS® are registered trademarks and Windows™ is a trademark of
Microsoft Corporation.

Acquisitions Editor: Dean Holmes
Project Editor: Nancy Siadek
Manuscript Editor: Eric Stroo
Technical Editor: Jim Fuchs

Contents

Introduction

This is your guide to MS-DOS, the Microsoft Disk Operating System, usually known as DOS. In particular, this book is about version 5 of DOS, the latest and most powerful version, developed for IBM and compatible personal computers.

In the following pages, you'll find out what DOS is, how you use it, and what's so special about version 5. The goal of the book is not to make you a "power user," but to make you comfortable with your computer and with DOS in most of the day-to-day situations you'll encounter. The book assumes no prior experience with DOS, but you shouldn't find its contents unnervingly simpleminded if you're already familiar with your computer.

DOS COMMANDS

The bulk of the book explains the commands you use to control DOS and, through it, your computer. Each chapter begins with a brief description of the subject—disks, files, devices, and so on—and then moves on to the most important DOS commands you need to work in that context.

Because DOS allows you to mold its commands, shaping them to suit a particular need, the book presents DOS commands in two different ways: the basic command form and examples showing how the command is used. The examples are easier to explain, so let's start with them. Whenever you see a line like this in an example:

```
C:\> format a:
```

the shaded characters show what you would type to issue the command to DOS.

The command form, called its *syntax,* is often more complicated than a specific example. It shows the command in general terms that make allowance for a whole range of possible ways to use the command. In command syntax, the following conventions help distinguish four major elements: characters you must type, information you must supply, information that's optional, and characters you can include to customize a command. The examples shown here illustrate these conventions with actual DOS commands, but don't worry about understanding what they mean. You'll know soon enough.

- Characters you must type are printed in normal type. Always include these. For example:

  dir

- Information you must supply is described in *italics*. For example:

  copy *source*

  When you type the command, replace *source* with the information that applies in the case at hand.

- Information that's optional is shown in *italics* and square brackets. For example:

  copy *source* [*destination*]

  If you decide to type in optional information, replace [*destination*] with the information that applies in the case at hand; do not type the square brackets.

- Optional characters, known as *switches,* that customize a command are shown exactly as you type them, including the initial slash character (/). For example:

  copy *source* [*destination*] /v

  If you compare the command forms shown in the book to those that DOS Help displays, you'll find that the book sometimes simplifies the syntax by presenting the command in the context of a particular task.

Questions? *To obtain further information about a new DOS installation, contact your hardware manufacturer or the appropriate resources in your corporation.*

CHAPTER 1

DOS and Your Computer

Note to the reader: This chapter is for beginning computer users and those who want to learn some basic facts about computers and DOS. If you are already familiar with these topics, you can skip to Chapter 2 for installation information or to Chapter 3, which begins the reference portion of the book.

Most people, as they approach computers for the first time, have a few questions: What exactly is a computer? How easily can I break it? Does it require any special care? Is it hard to use? What can it do? What is DOS, and what does *it* do? What are applications, and why do I need *them?*

Using a computer involves three basic items: the computer, some programs to help you do your work, and one special type of program called an *operating system.* This chapter introduces each member of the trio and shows how they are related to each other. The remaining chapters teach you about MS-DOS, your computer's operating system (hereafter called simply DOS). This book describes the commands through which DOS makes its capabilities available to you. As you will see, your computer's operating system and its commands enable you to start your applications, manage your files, and extend the reach of your computer to other devices, such as printers and modems.

As you learn more about DOS, you'll also begin to appreciate how much it constantly does for you—in the background. DOS assumes responsibility for a vital level of "unconscious" control over the parts of your computer system, much as parts of your nervous system are responsible for instincts and reflexes.

3

FIRST IMPRESSIONS

Stripped of accessories, such as a mouse and a printer, a computer consists of three main parts: a keyboard, a monitor, and the computer unit itself. Figure 1-1 shows a basic computer setup. When you turn the computer on (as described in Chapter 2), it goes through a startup routine that typically ends with characters like these on the screen:

C:\>

These characters are the DOS *prompt* and are your indication that DOS is available and waiting for your commands.

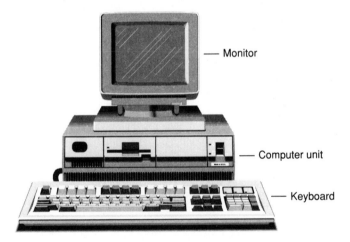

FIGURE 1-1. *A basic computer setup has three principal parts.*

WHAT IS A COMPUTER?

A computer is a machine that can do many different types of work. It can act as a fancy typewriter, helping you write letters; it can be a high-performance calculator, easing your work with budgets; it can be a fast-access notebook, keeping track of names and addresses; and it can be canvas and paintbrush or drafting table and pen, providing a versatile medium for decorative sketches or architectural drawings. A computer can be all these things and more, yet at heart it is still a machine over which you have total control.

You can break a computer if you try, but it's not particularly fragile. You don't want to drop it on the floor, shove it roughly around on your desk, or pile books and papers on top of it, but apart from taking some common-sense precautions, you'll find that a computer needs less care than your car in terms of maintenance and tune-ups:

- Keep it reasonably clean.

- Turn it off if you experience electrical problems, or if you anticipate them.

- Avoid extremes of heat and cold, either of which can damage its components or cause it to become unreliable.

- Be careful not to cover any air vents. Computers, like other electrical equipment, generate heat; the air vents let fresh air circulate inside the computer to keep it cool.

Otherwise, given normal, everyday use and normal, everyday care, your computer will run reliably for a long time, usually for years.

What Does It Do?

A computer does three types of work: It receives information, it processes (changes) that information in some way, and it gives you the results of the processing. These three tasks—*input, processing,* and *output*—are basically all that a computer does. If its workings seem more complex, it's because a computer is so very flexible in terms of the variety and quantity of information it can accept, the multitude of ways it can process that information, and the number of forms in which it can give you the results of its processing.

This flexibility contributes to the mystique of computers and the fascination they have for many people. No other machine can be used in so many different ways. The key to this flexibility comes from one characteristic all modern computers share: They are *interactive.* They respond to commands. You type one command, and the computer reacts immediately with an appropriate response. Type a different command, and the computer responds again, reacting in a different way to the new command. Instead of responding dumbly in a few predefined situations, a computer can respond with seeming intelligence, to the point of telling you on the spot whether it can or cannot carry out the command you just gave it, and whether it can do so immediately or only after you've provided more information.

Hardware plus Software

The computer itself, of course, doesn't do all this work on its own. The work is done by a combination of the computer, which is considered *hardware,* and sets of instructions, called *software,* or *computer programs.* Inside the machine, the instructions are interpreted and carried out to do the work you want to do. Although a computer can calculate far more quickly than any human, a computer without software is nothing more than an inert mass of metal and plastic. It can't do anything. On the other hand, software without a computer is simply wasted potential because only the computer can use the software and put it to work. It's this combination of machine and instructions that makes a computer so potent, so when you talk about a computer's being able to do this or that, remember that you're really referring to both the computer and its software. Specifically, you're referring to the software that accepts your commands and to the hardware that carries them out.

Parts of a Computer

As shown in Figure 1-1, a computer has three main parts, the *keyboard, computer unit,* and *monitor.* Together, these parts make up a working computer setup. Individually, the parts correspond closely to the three types of work a computer does:

- The keyboard is your primary means of entering information into the computer; it is the computer's main input device. Mice, joysticks, and trackballs are other types of input devices.

■ The computer unit is where the actual processing of information goes on; it contains the computer's microprocessor, its memory, and the associated chips and circuitry that contribute to processing information. On most computer setups, one or more disk drives are also located in the computer unit.

■ The monitor is where the computer displays the words and numbers you type, as well as the results of processing your information; it is the computer's primary output device. Printers, plotters, and modems are other types of output devices.

The Keyboard

The keyboard is your principal means of telling the computer what to do. A standard keyboard for an IBM PC computer (or a computer designed to be compatible with an IBM PC) has just over 100 keys. Many of these keys look and work like their equivalents on a typewriter or a calculator; others send commands to DOS or to an application.

One of the most striking differences between a typewriter and a computer keyboard, aside from the number of keys, is the way the computer's keys are grouped into several sets. The keys in the main portion of the keyboard are laid out like those of a standard typewriter, including letters of the alphabet, numbers, punctuation marks, and some special characters (such as $ and @). At the far right of the keyboard is a numeric keypad with a layout similar to that on a calculator. If you work with numbers a great deal, you can type them on the numeric keypad instead of using the less accessible number keys near the top of the keyboard.

The remaining keys don't have equivalents on a typewriter or calculator, but they are not difficult to learn. You use a number of these keys, either singly or in combination with other keys, in giving commands to DOS. The most important are described in the table on the following pages. These keys are labeled in Figure 1-2 on page 10. Don't worry about memorizing; examples later in the book tell you more about these and other keys as well.

IMPORTANT KEYS FOR CONTROLLING DOS

Key (or Combination)	Result for DOS
↵ Enter	Tells DOS you've finished typing a command and now want it to carry out the command. Until you press Enter, DOS waits for you to do something.
Esc	(Short for Escape) Your "cancel" key with DOS; before you press Enter, Esc lets you cancel a command you've been typing at the DOS prompt and start over.
⇧ Shift	Shifts the alphabetic and number keys from lowercase to uppercase. DOS doesn't normally distinguish between lowercase and uppercase characters, but it does assign significance to such characters as the asterisk (*) and the question mark (?), both of which you type with the Shift key.
Ctrl	(Short for Control) "Shifts" certain keys to give them a different meaning. As its name implies, Ctrl generally sends a program-control signal of some type to DOS or another program. Pressing Ctrl by itself doesn't cause anything to happen. For DOS-related functions of Ctrl, refer to Ctrl-Break and Ctrl-Alt-Del on the facing page.
Pause	Causes DOS to temporarily halt a long display to give you time to read what's on the screen; pressing any other key signals DOS to resume displaying more information. This key is usually labeled Pause on top and Break on the front. Its Break function in DOS comes into play only if you also press the Ctrl key, as described next.

IMPORTANT KEYS FOR CONTROLLING DOS

Key (or Combination)	Result for DOS

 Ctrl — Break

Tells DOS to stop and cancel whatever command it's carrying out. This is a key combination produced by holding down the Ctrl key and pressing the Break key. Like the Esc key, Ctrl-Break cancels a command, but it also stops and cancels a command you've already told DOS to carry out; Esc merely cancels a command you've typed but have not yet told DOS to carry out.

← Backspace

Moves the cursor one space to the left, at the same time erasing any character it moves over.

Num Lock

(Short for Numeric Lock) A toggle key, like a light switch, that shifts the numeric keypad between calculator-style numeric entry and cursor movement, as indicated by the arrows and words such as Home and End on the keys.

Ctrl — Alt — Del

Restarts the computer. This combination, difficult to press accidentally because it means holding down all three keys simultaneously, is important to remember for two reasons. First, restarting the computer means you *lose* all information that you have not yet saved on disk. There is no way to regain such lost information. On the plus side, Ctrl-Alt-Del is a quick way to start over in some situations, particularly if an application halts (hangs) your computer—a rare but possible occurrence—and you cannot break out of the program. Ctrl-Alt-Del is a way to escape in such situations, even though it means losing any unsaved work.

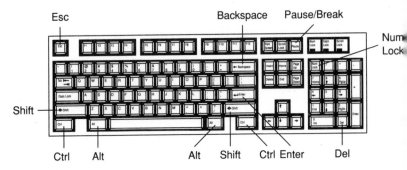

FIGURE 1-2. *A standard computer keyboard.*

A number of other keys, such as Home, End, Page Up, Page Down, and the function keys (labeled F1, F2, F3, and so on) either aren't as important to DOS as those in the table or aren't used by DOS at all. Some of these keys are mentioned later; the remainder often have significant roles to play in applications, such as word processors and spreadsheets. The manuals for such applications give you details on how and when to use these keys.

The Computer Unit

Although the computer unit is the most important part of your setup, it is also the part you least need to try to understand—unless you like delving into such matters. Computer people sometimes use the term *black box* to refer to a piece of hardware that takes input and works in some mysterious way to process it and produce output. If you want, you can think of your computer unit as a type of black box: You feed it input, and it produces output.

Although you don't have to know anything about how your computer works internally, you should be able to identify one part of it: the microprocessor. Sometimes called the CPU (for central processing unit), the microprocessor is a complex network of silicon circuitry housed in a square or rectangular package an inch or two on a side. Small though it is, the microprocessor is the most vital of your computer's internal "organs" because it is the part of your computer that computes—through it pass all the words and numbers that go into producing your reports, budgets, forecasts, mailing lists, and other documents.

An IBM PC–compatible computer is based on one of
several microprocessors developed by Intel Corporation.
Known collectively as members of the 80x86 series, these
microprocessors and the types of computers with which
they are most commonly identified are presented in the
table that follows.

Microprocessor	Computer
8086/8088	IBM PC, IBM PC/XT, and compatibles
80286	IBM PC/AT and compatibles
80386, 80386SX	High-end personal computers, such as the IBM PS/2 Model 80
i486, i486SX	High-performance engineering workstations and comparable computers

Together, the microprocessors in this table form a
family that has evolved since 1980–81, when the first IBM
PC was developed and released. Newer members of the
family are identified by higher numbers in the series—for
example, the 80386 is newer than the 80286. The microprocessors differ in speed, in the amount of information they
can work with at one time, in the amount of memory they
can use, and in the ways they work with your programs.
All, however, work with DOS.

The Monitor

Work in a computer happens inside the computer unit
where you can't see it. But the computer, being an interactive machine, needs a way for its programs to show you
the current state of affairs, ask you for instructions, and no-
tify you of problems. That way, of course, is the monitor.
As you work with a computer, the screen acts as your window into the computer's workplace. Because events inside
the computer are ever changing, the display on-screen isn't
static either. It changes constantly to show you the latest
happenings—even so small an event as your typing a period or pressing the Spacebar.

Because a screen can rapidly become full of information, you must be able to tell where your typing will
appear. The computer relays this information by means of
a blinking underline called the *cursor*. No matter how much
information is on the screen, the cursor represents the place

where your next typed character will be displayed. For example, the DOS prompt mentioned earlier has the following on-screen appearance:

```
C:\>_
```

When you see the cursor, you know that whatever character you type will appear at that place on the screen. As you type, the cursor continually moves one space to the right, always remaining just ahead of the last typed character. (If you type enough characters to move the cursor past the right edge of the screen, the cursor "wraps"; that is, it moves to the left edge of the next line.)

MEMORY AND DISK STORAGE

Computers contain a certain amount of short-term memory, known as *random access memory,* or *RAM*. Your computer uses RAM to hold calculations and whatever information it (the computer) needs to access quickly. DOS is in RAM, the application you're currently using is in RAM, and most important, your data is in RAM.

Most IBM PC–compatible computers these days have either 640 kilobytes (640 KB) or 1 megabyte (1 MB) of RAM. These amounts are enough to hold, respectively, about 640,000 or 1,000,000 characters of information—seemingly a respectable amount. RAM, however, can hold information only so long as the computer is kept turned on. As soon as you turn the computer off or restart it by pressing Ctrl-Alt-Del, the contents of RAM disappear.

To save information for future use, your computer uses storage devices—*disks*—which have surfaces that can be recorded on and erased like the recording tape in a cassette. All programs and data you want to save for future use with your computer must be stored on disk.

Organizing and saving information on disk is much like doing the same with papers on your desktop. Whether those papers are scrawled notes or long, carefully prepared reports, each paper is a separate document. If you want, you can pencil an identifying label on each piece of paper: "Budget Meeting" on one, for example, and "Call to Jake" on another. When you save the documents you want to keep for later reference, you put them in a file cabinet, organized in file folders.

With a computer, you do the same thing, only your file cabinet is a disk, and your documents and file folders are electronic. Suppose you create a document on your computer; no matter how short or preliminary the document might be, if you want to save it, you give it a name and save it on disk. The name you assign becomes the document's *filename*. This filename is the way you tell DOS and your other programs which document you want to use.

Disks and How They Work

Disks for computers come in two main types, *floppy* (removable) and *hard* (nonremovable). Whether hard or floppy, a computer disk is essentially a round, flat, recordlike object coated with a thin layer of magnetic material. This coating is the part of the disk that actually holds information. Whether you use the disk to store a letter, a budget, or a digitized reproduction of Whistler's mother, the information is coded magnetically onto the surface of the disk. To record (*write*) on or retrieve (*read*) from a disk, your disk drive relies on one or more mechanisms called *read/write heads,* each of which moves across and slightly above the surface of the disk like the arm on a record player. When a disk is in use, it spins rapidly inside the disk drive, with the read/write heads moving between the outer rim and the center of the disk.

Read/write heads encode information on the magnetic surface when they write, and they detect previously coded information when they read. The coding itself remains on the disk's surface until you either erase it or record over it. Thus, whatever information you transfer from your computer's memory to disk is a permanent record of whatever work you were doing with your computer.

Caution: *Remember that information is recorded magnetically on computer disks. Be careful to keep floppy disks in particular away from magnetic items on your desktop. Bringing a disk into contact with a magnet or running it through a cassette-tape eraser is an excellent way to damage or destroy the information it contains.*

Because their magnetic surfaces are easily scratched and are sensitive to dust and other contaminants, all computer disks are encased in some type of protective housing. In the case of a hard disk, one or more metal disks called *platters* are mounted on a central spindle and completely enclosed, with their read/write heads, in an airtight metal and plastic box. A hard disk is usually fixed inside the computer unit and is capable of holding vast quantities of information— 60, 80, 100 million characters and more. If you have a hard disk, be careful not to jar the computer when the disk is in use; you could damage either your data or the disk itself.

Floppy Disks

Floppy disks are lightweight and portable. (Contrary to their name, however, floppy disks aren't meant to be bendable.) When you want the computer to read information from a floppy disk or write information on it, you place the disk in your floppy disk drive. To insert the disk, you hold it face up, with the label (or the space where a label is to go) under your thumb. When not in use, floppy disks should be stored in a container made for them or in some other place where they are safe from damaging influence— dust, scratches, dampness, temperature extremes, magnetic objects, and the like.

Floppy disks are available in two sizes, 5¼-inch and 3½-inch, as illustrated in Figure 1-3. Floppy disk drives are designed to use one or the other, but not both, disk sizes. The 5¼-inch disks are larger, flatter, and floppier, and they have a large hole in the center that fits around the disk's

5¼-inch disk   3½-inch disk

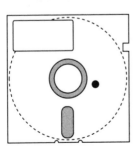
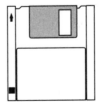

FIGURE 1-3. *Floppy disks.*

drive mechanism. The 3½-inch disks are rigid, with a smaller opening in the middle and a metal "shutter" that opens when the disk is in use. Floppy disks, especially the 3½-inch ones, are relatively sturdy, but you should still be careful with them. The 5¼-inch disks make terrific frisbees, but don't assume that their contents will survive the flight.

Floppy disks, like hard disks, come in a range of *disk capacities*. Your floppy disk drive is designed to work by default with disks that can hold a specific amount of information, so you should know which disk capacity works best with the disk drive.

Shared Disks

The ability to share information is one of the great advantages of working with a computer. The most obvious means of sharing are sending a copy of your work to a printer and, if you're so inclined, connecting your computer to other computers with the help of a communications device called a *modem*. These devices and the ways in which they're used with DOS are described in Chapter 6.

If you work in an office with many connected computers, however, you know there is yet another way to share information: a local area network, or LAN. Computers on a network can pass information back and forth. More than that, they often share a single resource, such as a large hard disk or a printer. In the case of a shared hard disk, the computers connected to it can use the disk as if it were literally a part of themselves. Thanks to the network connection and network software, the computers "see" no difference between a hard disk on the desktop and a network disk that's physically located several doors away or even in the next building. Furthermore, the network disk can be set up so that individual portions of storage space can be dedicated for use by only one person, by a group of people, or by anyone with access to the network.

Use of a network is far too large a topic for such a small book as this, but at a minimum you will find it helpful to know that DOS can and does work with disks, printers, and other devices on a network, although in situations where you could conceivably alter other people's data, DOS places limits on what you can do with a shared resource. If you use a network and want to know more about it, contact the person designated as your network administrator.

TYPES OF SOFTWARE

As mentioned at the beginning of this section, software gives your computer the ability to perform useful work. In effect, software wakes up the machine and makes it responsive to your commands. A computer runs two basic types of software, an operating system and applications. DOS is an operating system. Word processors, spreadsheets, games, and other programs that "do something useful" are applications—they apply the computer's abilities to a particular task or group of tasks.

DOS and What It Does

DOS stands for Disk Operating System, and it refers to a set of programs that manage computer operations. Some of the operations DOS controls are not even visible to you, but many others are both visible and important because they are related to finding and saving the information you work with—the words and numbers that make up the data you want to store, print, or send to someone else.

DOS can be, and is, commonly described by analogy: traffic cop, symphony conductor, circus ringmaster. All of these analogies point out the role it plays as system superintendent of your computer. It is DOS that maintains order, stores and retrieves information, and ensures that parts of the computer setup work smoothly together and with your applications.

Versions of DOS

When you purchase DOS, you receive a set of disks that contain one particular version of DOS. Since its release in 1981, DOS has grown to match hardware and software developments and to keep pace with the ever-expanding needs of its users. Each new DOS release is given a number, to identify it uniquely in the DOS lineage. The first DOS was version 1; succeeding major releases were numbered 2, 3, and 4. Within each major release have come less significant updates; these are identified as decimal numbers, for example, version 2.1 and version 3.3. The version on which this reference is based, version 5.0, is the newest, most powerful, and most efficient version of DOS available.

Regardless of version number, however, the disks you receive when you purchase DOS are simply disks. They hold the many parts of DOS, but before you can use your computer, you or someone else must install DOS on the hard disk or on floppy disks. Only then can your computer find and use your operating system, and only then can you really put your computer to work. If you have yet to install DOS, Chapter 2 tells you how to go about doing so.

Internal and External Commands

When you use DOS, you are actually using a set of programs. Some of these programs remain in your computer's memory at all times, regardless of other work you might be doing. Other, less essential parts of DOS remain on disk, available when your computer needs them but not consuming memory you might need for applications, such as your word processing program.

Those parts of DOS that remain on disk until needed are known as *external* commands; those parts that reside in memory are *internal* commands. Although some are external and others are internal, all DOS commands are used the same way. If DOS is on your hard disk, you'll notice the external commands mostly because the light on your hard disk comes on when DOS goes to the disk to find them.

If you're using DOS from floppy disks, however, the difference between external and internal commands becomes more significant. If you try to use an external command that DOS can't find on the disk it's currently using, DOS responds *Bad command or file name.* Your command isn't bad. DOS simply couldn't find it. Insert a different DOS disk and try again, or, as described in Chapter 3,

print a list of the files on each of your DOS disks and keep
it close by for quick reference.

Windows and Other Environments

As you can see, you are using not one, but two and perhaps
more types of software when you use a computer. These
types of software work closely together, each performing
the task it is designed to do. When you picture your computer at work, think of a pyramid. The pyramid rests on a
hardware platform that represents your computer setup.
Within this pyramid is your software, arranged in layers as
shown in Figure 1-4.

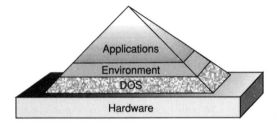

FIGURE 1-4. *Layers of software in a computer.*

At the bottom of the software pyramid, taking care of
all basic functions, is DOS. Although DOS is software, it's
software of a special type that works very closely with the
hardware, translating your commands and those of your applications into instructions that the hardware can carry out.

Above DOS is a second layer, which you might or might
not use on your computer. Not really an integral part of the
operating system and not quite an application, this layer
provides you with a work environment, for example, the environment provided by Microsoft Windows or that displayed by the DOS Shell. Basically, the environment acts
as an intermediary between DOS, your applications, and
you to provide a consistent and predictable *interface:* You
know what to expect, and once you've gotten familiar with
the terrain, you can easily learn to maneuver. Although you
can't use such an operating environment without DOS, you
can run DOS without the environment.

At the top of the pyramid are your applications—word processors, spreadsheets, database managers, drawing packages. These applications are the most visible and the most immediately useful software on your computer. They rely on DOS and, in some instances, on Windows or some other operating environment you run on your computer. Applications help you make your computer productive, but in order to function, they need the services provided by DOS. You can run DOS without running applications. You can run DOS and an operating environment without applications. But you can't run applications without DOS and, in some cases, without Windows or another environment in which the applications are designed to work.

CHAPTER 2

Installing and Starting DOS

Although installing DOS might sound tricky, it isn't. DOS comes with its own installation program, named Setup, so for a basic installation you don't have to know much more than how to place a floppy disk in your disk drive and where to find the Enter key and the direction keys on your keyboard. Setup does the rest.

A FEW NOTES ABOUT SETUP

The files on your DOS disks are stored in a special compressed format that must be decompressed, or expanded, before you can use DOS. Setup performs this backstage magic during installation, so be sure to use the Setup program, even if you've managed to install earlier versions of DOS simply by copying files from one disk to another. For all the work it does behind the scenes, Setup has been designed with user friendliness in mind. Setup:

■ Offers help whenever you need it. During installation, you can press the F1 key to request more information about whatever Setup is doing at the time. When you press F1, installation stops temporarily, and Setup displays an explanation on the screen, waiting for you to press a key before it continues.

■ Asks whether you want DOS to run the DOS Shell whenever you start your system. The Shell is a work environment that many hardware manufacturers include with the operating system. The Shell comes complete with menus and graphical elements that make using DOS easier in many ways. If you aren't certain you want to use it, you can choose not to have DOS run the Shell at startup. (You can always run it from the DOS prompt, as described in Chapter 9.)

■ Shows you what's happening every step of the way. It tells you what percentage of the installation is complete and displays messages that tell you what Setup is doing.

The Setup program occasionally refers to the *Microsoft MS-DOS Getting Started* and *Microsoft MS-DOS User's Guide and Reference* manuals. If you need additional help at these times, see the manuals if you have access to them or contact your hardware manufacturer.

On most systems, especially new ones or those with standard accessories, installation should present little difficulty and no subsequent problems with DOS. If you use nonstandard accessories or experience problems using hardware or software after DOS is installed, check the file named README.TXT in your DOS directory before calling your dealer or other resources. To see the contents of the file, type the following command at the DOS prompt:

```
C:\> type c:\dos\readme.txt ¦ more
```

This command displays the contents of the file, one screenful of information at a time. Press any key to see the next screenful of information. To print the contents of the file, type the following command at the DOS prompt:

```
C:\> copy c:\dos\readme.txt prn
```

WHERE TO GO FROM HERE

DOS can be installed on a hard disk or on floppy disks. If your computer dealer has already installed DOS on your computer, you can skip the installation instructions and move ahead to the explanation of your computer's startup routine, under the heading ''Startup.'' For details about checking to see whether DOS is already installed and about the procedures for installing DOS, refer to the sections identified on the following page.

- "Checking for DOS" if you have a computer with a hard disk and don't know whether DOS is already installed and ready to use

- "Installing DOS" if you are installing DOS on a hard disk for the first time

- "Installing DOS on Floppy Disks" if you need to create a working copy of DOS on floppy disks

CHECKING FOR DOS

Note on this section: This topic applies only to computers with hard disks. If your computer doesn't have a hard disk, there's no need to check for DOS because you must insert a DOS disk into drive A to start or restart the computer.

If you have a computer with a hard disk, but you don't know whether DOS has already been installed on it, check for DOS by removing any floppy disks and starting your computer. If you see a string of messages followed by this prompt:

```
C:\>
```

a version of DOS is already installed on your computer's hard disk. Skip the installation instructions and move ahead to the explanation of your computer's startup routine, under the heading "Startup."

If, on starting your computer, you don't see the DOS prompt but you do see a display of lists or graphics (or both), you too can assume that DOS is installed. In your case, part of the startup routine tells DOS to start another program, such as the DOS Shell (shown on the opposite page), Microsoft Windows, or some other work environment. Skip to the heading "Startup."

If DOS Is Not Installed

If you start your computer and see the message *Non-System disk or disk error*, your computer cannot find the part of DOS that it needs to get started, so you probably have to install DOS on your hard disk. (A disk needs several special DOS files to be able to start a computer. A non-system disk

```
                              MS-DOS Shell
 File  Options  View  Tree  Help
 C:\
 [A:]  [B:]  [C:]  [D:]

          Directory Tree                        C:\*.*
 [-] C:\                          ▶ AUTOEXEC.BAT        54  06-24-91
   ├─[ ] DOS                        COMMAND .COM    47,845  04-09-91
   └─[ ] TOOLS                      CONFIG  .SYS       113  06-24-91
                                    MIRROR  .FIL    61,952  06-21-91
                                    WINA20  .386     9,349  04-09-91



                                Main
 Command Prompt
 Editor
 MS-DOS QBasic
 [Disk Utilities]


 F10=Actions  Shift+F9=Command Prompt                        1:22p
```

doesn't contain these files.) Before turning to the appropriate installation instructions, however, first check to be sure that drive A is empty or at least that the drive latch is open.

Although the *Non-System disk* message does appear when DOS hasn't been installed, it also appears any time you mistakenly place a non-system disk in drive A, close the latch (or push a 3½-inch disk into position), and then start or restart your computer. If a disk in drive A is not the cause of the error message, go to "Installing DOS," below. You can ignore the message itself for a while; you won't hurt anything.

INSTALLING DOS

For a new installation onto a hard disk, all you need are your original DOS disks. If your hard disk has already been prepared for DOS, the installation takes just a few minutes. If your hard disk has not yet been prepared, the installation performs the necessary steps, but the process takes more time—commonly several additional minutes.

To start installation:

■ If your computer is not running, place the DOS disk labeled Disk 1 in drive A. Close the drive latch and turn on your computer.

■ If your computer is running, place Disk 1 in drive A, close the drive latch, and press Ctrl-Alt-Del to restart your computer.

Either of these methods takes you directly into the Setup program. Some opening messages appear on the screen, telling you what to expect from Setup, what it has determined about your computer, and how to proceed. From this point on, follow the instructions that Setup displays, changing the DOS disks in drive A as Setup asks for each of the original DOS disks. Remember that if you have questions or need more information, you can always press the F1 key for help. When the installation is complete, follow Setup's instructions to restart your computer. DOS will then be running and ready to go to work. Skip ahead now to the section headed "Startup."

INSTALLING DOS ON FLOPPY DISKS

You can install DOS on floppy disks whether or not your computer has a hard disk, but if you have a choice, install DOS on your hard disk. Your computer will be much easier to use than if you try to work from floppies.

For the installation, you need several blank floppy disks that can be used in your startup drive (drive A). Use the following list as a guide and label the disks as indicated. If you have two floppy disk drives, you can speed up installation by using one for the DOS disks and the other for your blank disks, even if the two drives are of different capacities. Be sure, however, that the disks onto which you install DOS can be read by drive A.

Startup Drive	Blank Disks	Suggested Labels
1.2-MB or 1.44-MB	3 (5¼" 1.2-MB) or 3 (3½" 1.44-MB)	Startup/Support/Shell, Help/Basic/Edit/Utility, Supplemental
720-KB	4 (3½" 720-KB or 1.44-MB)	Startup/Support, Shell/Help, Basic/Edit/Utility, Supplemental
360-KB	7 (5¼" 360-KB)	Startup, Support, Shell, Help, Basic/Edit, Utility, Supplemental

To install DOS, start your computer and place the DOS disk labeled Disk 1 in a compatible floppy drive. Close the drive latch if necessary. Next:

1. If you have the DOS disks for a new installation, restart your computer by pressing Ctrl-Alt-Del.

   If you have the upgrade disks instead, type *x:setup /f,* substituting for *x* the letter of the drive containing the DOS disk. Skip to step 3.

2. Start your computer, or restart it by pressing the key combination Ctrl-Alt-Del.

3. After Setup checks your computer and presents some opening messages, it displays a box containing a list of default (assumed) settings. The last item in this list reads *Install To:.* If necessary, use the Up direction key and the Enter key as described on the screen to change the setting from *Hard disk* to *Floppy disks.*

4. Follow the setup instructions as they appear. Remember that you can request help with the F1 key.

STARTUP

When you turn on the computer's power switch, a number of events take place, all of which contribute to the process known as a *cold boot,* or *booting* the computer. (If your computer doesn't have a hard disk, put your startup disk in drive A before you turn on the computer.) As you would expect, the term *booting* comes from the adage about pulling yourself up by your bootstraps, and it's appropriate because the computer essentially wakes itself up and pulls itself into shape. (When you press Ctrl-Alt-Del to restart the computer, you perform a *warm boot,* or *reboot* the system, a process that skips most of the hardware checks described below.)

In a cold boot, as power begins to flow through the machine, your computer checks for, and reads into memory, a set of permanently recorded instructions that tell it what to do first. The computer then begins to check itself, along with its memory, disk drives, and keyboard. This is happening when you hear your computer whir, grunt to itself, and beep, and when you see lights flash on your keyboard and disk drives.

Once it finds all its parts and determines that they are in working order, the computer checks for DOS. This happens both when you boot and when you reboot the computer.

The first place the computer checks is drive A, a practice that dates back to the time when many computers had no more than one floppy disk drive. Because so many computers now have a hard disk, the computer then goes to drive C—if and only if drive A is empty (or unlatched).

If drive A contains a disk, the computer attempts to find several special DOS files on it. Failing that, the machine symbolically shrugs its shoulders, tells you *Non-System disk or disk error*, and asks for a new, acceptable disk that does contain the DOS files it needs. Leave drive A empty (or unlatched) if you're trying to start the computer from your hard disk.

After the computer finds the DOS files and reads them into memory, messages start to appear on the screen. Most of these messages are simply status reports; even if they report ''errors,'' they require no response from you.

The DOS Prompt

When DOS is ready to go to work, startup ends, and the DOS prompt appears on the screen. The DOS Setup program sets the prompt to look like this:

```
C:\>
```

If your prompt looks different, DOS has been instructed to display a different prompt. Regardless, you should see the blinking underline, or cursor, that tells you DOS is waiting for you to tell it what to do.

If you don't see a DOS prompt at all, you see instead the ''face'' of a program that overlies DOS and helps make your computer easier to use. Such programs include the DOS Shell (illustrated earlier and described in Chapter 9) and Microsoft Windows, as well as many other programs designed for the same purpose.

Special Startup Instructions: CONFIG.SYS and AUTOEXEC.BAT

Once your computer finds DOS and reads it into memory, control passes to DOS. Before it displays the C:\> prompt, DOS itself performs one final startup task: It checks for two special lists of instructions, which are stored in files named CONFIG.SYS and AUTOEXEC.BAT. The DOS Setup program creates both the CONFIG.SYS and AUTOEXEC.BAT files for you when it installs DOS.

As you learn more about DOS, the names of these two files will crop up often. But even when you know nothing about computers or DOS, you see these files and their results every time you start your computer.

In brief, CONFIG.SYS contains instructions that *configure* DOS to work with your computer. The commands in AUTOEXEC.BAT are simply DOS commands that you routinely want DOS to execute at startup. Placing such commands in AUTOEXEC.BAT is a timesaving way to make your computer more personal—more comfortable and better geared to the way you work and the things you do.

Chapter 7 tells you about commands you can use in CONFIG.SYS and AUTOEXEC.BAT, and shows you how to put them there.

TYPING DOS COMMANDS

CONFIG.SYS and AUTOEXEC.BAT contain ''pretyped'' commands that DOS reads and carries out. In your work with DOS and your computer, however, you will generally type commands directly at the keyboard.

Whenever you give DOS a command, you type it and press the Enter key. Until you press Enter, DOS waits for more keystrokes, so think of Enter as your means of telling DOS to get to work. For example, DOS includes a command called Memory (abbreviated Mem) that allows you to check on the amount of available memory in your system.

To use the command, you would type it in the following shorthand form:

```
C:\> mem
```

and then press Enter. If you try this yourself, you see a report on your computer's memory similar to this:

```
655360 bytes total conventional memory
655360 bytes available to MS-DOS
593856 largest executable program size
```

(Chapter 8 tells you about this report; right now, think of Memory as simply an example of a DOS command.)

Like most programs, DOS takes your commands very literally. If you mistype a command, DOS doesn't have the ability to guess what you meant to type. If you see the error before you press Enter, press the Esc key or backspace to the problem, and then retype the command.

On the other hand, if you don't spot the error before pressing the Enter key, DOS tells you it doesn't recognize what you typed. For example, suppose you type *mom* instead of *mem*:

```
C:\> mom
```

After you press Enter, DOS responds

```
Bad command or file name
```

and redisplays its prompt:

```
C:\>
```

You won't have done anything wrong, and you won't have broken DOS; you will merely have given it a command it could not interpret. To complete the command, retype it (correcting any spelling errors) and press Enter.

Note to floppy disk users: *Chapter 1 explained that DOS includes two types of commands, internal and external. If you have more than one DOS disk, remember that you see the message* Bad command or file name *when you try to use an external command that is not on the DOS disk you're using. Before losing your temper or demanding a typewriter, try the command with your other DOS disks.*

SOME BASIC DOS COMMANDS

The remainder of this chapter introduces some basic DOS commands. If you want to try them, type the commands shown in the examples. The part you type always appears shaded in the sample command line. The computer's response is shown after each command so that you'll know what you should see. The same format is used throughout the book for presenting examples.

Note to the reader: The examples provide guidance in using
DOS commands, but feel free to try your own variations—
that's almost always the best way to learn. But exercise a little
caution before you find yourself exercising 20/20 hindsight.
Stop and think before you experiment with a command that
can affect valuable programs or data. Better yet, try your
variations on expendable files, such as those you've duplicated on a floppy disk with the Copy command, described in
Chapter 5.

If you want to try some commands but your computer is
displaying the DOS Shell, press the F3 key to exit the Shell
and return to the DOS prompt. If your computer is displaying Windows, press the Alt and F4 keys at the same time
(Alt-F4) to quit, and then press Enter to confirm your in-
tention when Windows tells you it's about to exit. If your
computer is running a different shell or operating environment, use whatever command is needed to quit and return
to the DOS prompt.

Changing Drives

Each of the drives on your computer is identified by a different letter. To DOS, your first floppy disk drive is A;
your second floppy drive, if you have one, is B; your hard
disk is C. If you have only one floppy disk drive, DOS can
use it as either A or B when you type commands. Additional drives, such as a second hard disk or a network drive,
are D, E, F, and so on, up to a possible drive Z.

When you start DOS, it uses one of your disk drives as
the *current,* or *active,* drive, the one containing the disk and
files it will use in carrying out your commands. If you start
your computer from a floppy disk, the current drive is A. If
you start from a hard disk, the current drive is C. Unless it
has been customized in some way, your DOS prompt identifies the current drive. If your DOS prompt is *C:\>*, for example, your current drive is indicated by the characters *C:*
in the prompt. (You can ignore the backslash until you start
dividing disks into directories, as described in Chapter 5.)

Unless you modify a command to indicate otherwise,
DOS applies the command to the current drive. Because

most computers have more than one disk drive, however, DOS lets you change the current drive by typing the letter of the drive you want to use, followed by a colon (:). For example, if C is the current drive and you want to use drive A, you type

```
C:\> a:
```

The DOS prompt changes from *C:\>* to *A:\>* to show that the current drive is A, and all succeeding commands you type will affect the disk in drive A—unless you specify otherwise by using the drive letter (always followed by a colon) in the command. Examples and command descriptions in later parts of this book show you how and when you can include drive letters in commands.

To change the current drive back to C, you type

```
A:\> c:
```

Requesting Help

DOS responds to a sizable number of commands, many of which can be customized with drive letters, the names of files, and other optional characters that refine the way commands are carried out. To help you sort out these commands, version 5 of DOS, unlike any earlier version, has a feature called *online Help*. This feature does not teach you how to use DOS, but it's a great time-saver when you want to see what a particular command does or how to use it.

To request a list of DOS commands, along with a brief description of each, you type

```
C:\> help
```

DOS responds with the first of several screenfuls of information, the first few lines of which are shown on the opposite page. Press any key to see the next screenful of information, or press Ctrl-Break (hold down the Ctrl key and press Break) to interrupt the series of Help screens and return to the DOS prompt.

More often than not, you'll use Help to request information on a specific command—in either of the ways shown on the opposite page. The examples use the Version command,

```
APPEND    Allows programs to open data files in specified directories as if
          they were in the current directory.
ASSIGN    Redirects requests for disk operations on one drive to a different
          drive.
ATTRIB    Displays or changes file attributes.
BACKUP    Backs up one or more files from one disk to another.
BREAK     Sets or clears extended CTRL+C checking.
CALL      Calls one batch program from another.
CD        Displays the name of or changes the current directory.
CHCP      Displays or sets the active code page number.
CHDIR     Displays the name of or changes the current directory.
CHKDSK    Checks a disk and displays a status report.
CLS       Clears the screen.
COMMAND   Starts a new instance of the MS-DOS command interpreter.
COMP      Compares the contents of two files or sets of files.
COPY      Copies one or more files to another location.
CTTY      Changes the terminal device used to control your system.
DATE      Displays or sets the date.
DEBUG     Runs Debug, a program testing and editing tool.
DEL       Deletes one or more files.
DIR       Displays a list of files and subdirectories in a directory.
DISKCOMP  Compares the contents of two floppy disks.
DISKCOPY  Copies the contents of one floppy disk to another.
DOSKEY    Edits command lines, recalls MS-DOS commands, and creates macros.
-- More --
```

abbreviated Ver, which tells you the version of DOS you're using.

To request help on a particular command, you can type *help*, followed by the name of the command:

```
C:\> help ver
```

To save a few keystrokes, you can, instead, type the command name followed by a slash (/) and a question mark:

```
C:\> ver /?
```

Either request causes DOS to produce the following report:

```
Displays the MS-DOS version.

VER
```

The first line, *Displays the MS-DOS version*, tells you what the command does. The second, *VER*, shows what you type to use the command. The Version command is very simple; with other DOS commands you can include *switches* (characters that modify the command) and optional information, such as the names of files. Help for those commands is more detailed.

The Date and Time Commands

Although your computer most likely keeps the date and time current for you, you can use the Date and Time commands if you ever want or need to change the date and time of day that DOS uses. To change the date, you type the Date command:

```
C:\> date
```

DOS displays the date and waits for you to type a new one:

```
Current date is Thu 07-04-1991
Enter new date (mm-dd-yy): _
```

To respond, you type the date in the form shown in the command: numbers for the month, day, and year separated by hyphens. For example, to set the date to December 4, 1991, type the shaded characters and press Enter:

```
Current date is Thu 07-04-1991
Enter new date (mm-dd-yy) 12-4-91
```

To save a little time, you can also set the date in a single command. Type *date*, followed by the date you want to set:

```
C:\> date 12-4-91
```

The Time command is comparable in all ways to the Date command except for the form in which you type the current time. Thus, you can let DOS prompt you for the new time, as follows:

```
C:\> time
Current time is  3:00:52.34p
Enter new time: 12:11p
```

Or you can simply type

```
C:\> time 12:11p
```

Enter the time in hours and minutes (seconds being rather difficult), and separate the numbers with colons, as shown in the example. You can use either a 24-hour format (0 through 23 for the hours from midnight through 11 p.m.) or a 12-hour format (0 through 12 noon and 1 through 11 p.m.). If you opt for the 12-hour format, be sure to follow the time with *a* for a.m. or *p* for p.m., as shown above.

The Clear Screen Command

As you work with DOS and give it one command after another, your screen becomes cluttered with information. Although the DOS prompt and the cursor always tell you where your next command will be displayed, you'll sometimes find it helpful to begin typing a set of commands on a blank screen. The DOS Clear Screen command wipes the screen and gives you a ''blank slate'' on which to work. To clear the screen, you must type the command in its abbreviated form:

```
C:\> cls
```

When you press Enter, the screen clears, and DOS displays the prompt in the upper left corner.

The Doskey Command

Doskey is the name of a version 5 command that loads a small program into your computer's memory. Once loaded, Doskey sits in the background, tracking the commands you type and storing them in a temporary storage area called a *buffer*. If you type the same command over and over, or if you repeat commands with small variations (for example, *dir a:* one time, *dir c:* the next), Doskey can help you save time and keystrokes by retrieving earlier commands from its buffer and redisplaying the one you choose. Pressing the Enter key then tells DOS to carry out the command again, without your having to retype it.

To start Doskey, you type its name:

```
C:\> doskey
```

DOS responds with the message

```
DOSKey installed.
```

Doskey is now operating in the background to keep track of the commands you type.

The examples that follow illustrate simple uses of Doskey to reuse and review previous commands. The examples assume that you have entered the series of DOS commands shown at the top of the next page.

```
C:\> ver
C:\> dir
C:\> cls
C:\> date 12-25-91
C:\> time 8:00a
```

Reusing a Command

To redisplay a command, press the Up direction key once
for each command in the list, going from latest to earliest.
Within the list, you can move to a later command by pressing the Down direction key. To carry out the command
again, you press Enter. So, for example, pressing the
Up direction key four times with the sample shown above
would ultimately cause Doskey to display

```
C:\>dir
```

Pressing the Down direction key once would change the
display to

```
C:\>cls
```

and pressing Enter at this point would cause DOS to carry
out the Clear Screen command again.

You can also press the keys labeled Page Up (or PgUp)
and Page Down (PgDn) to move to the beginning or end of
the list (if the Num Lock light on your keyboard is off).

Listing Earlier Commands

Doskey can normally keep track of several dozen commands. After you've used so many, however, pressing the
Up direction key can be a bothersome way to repeat a command you last used quite a while ago. To make finding a
command easier, you can press the F7 key to see all the
commands you've entered, starting with the earliest commands in Doskey's list. When you press F7, Doskey numbers and displays the commands in order:

```
1: ver
2: dir
3: cls
4: date 12-25-91
5: time 8:00a
```

If you've entered too many commands to fit on a single screen, the display stops at one screenful and you see --*More*-- at the bottom. This tells you that the buffer contains more commands. To see them, press any key. To avoid seeing the rest of the commands, press Ctrl-Break.

After you list the commands in Doskey's buffer, you can use the direction keys to move up or down in the list to display the command you want. If the list is long, however, it's better to remember the number of the command and ask for that command by number.

Reusing a Particular Command

If you know the number of the command you want to reuse, you can redisplay it immediately by pressing the F9 key. If, for example, you wanted to reuse the Clear Screen command (number 3 in the sample list), pressing F9 would cause Doskey to display

```
C:\>Line number:
```

Typing *3* and pressing Enter would produce this:

```
C:\>cls
```

and pressing Enter again would clear the screen.

The preceding description of Doskey covers only the basics of starting the program and retrieving commands. As your use of DOS expands, you will want to explore Doskey options that let you edit the commands you retrieve and save them as a group in batch files or macros.

CHAPTER 3

Disks

Because disks are so important to using and managing data with your computer, DOS includes a number of disk-related commands. This chapter describes the following DOS commands:

- Format, for preparing disks for use; Volume and Label, for naming disks

- Check Disk, for checking the condition of and available storage on a disk

- Diskcopy, for copying an entire disk

- Diskcomp, for comparing two floppy disks

- Mirror, for saving information about a disk and the files it contains

- Unformat, for recovering files on an accidentally reformatted disk

All the information—DOS, applications, and data—that you save for future use on your computer is stored on disk. If you have a hard disk, you'll probably store DOS on it, and you'll also use it to store your applications and most or all of your data. If you don't have a hard disk, you'll use copies of your program disks for starting your applications, and you'll use data disks for saving your files.

THE STRUCTURE OF A DISK

All DOS disks are organized in the same basic way, as shown in Figure 3-1. As shown, every disk has two *sides*. Both of these are normally used for storage, so DOS

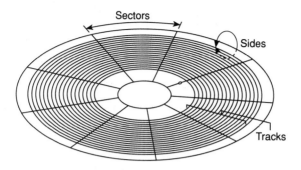

FIGURE 3-1. *Organization of a disk.*

distinguishes one from the other by referring to them by
number. On a floppy disk, the upper surface is side 0, and
the lower surface is side 1.

On each side, a disk is divided into circular regions
called *tracks.* The number of tracks on any particular disk
depends on its storage capacity; a floppy disk has either 40
or 80 tracks per side. Each track on each side of a disk is
further divided into segments called *sectors,* each of which
can hold a certain predetermined amount of information.

If they were visible on the disk's surface, tracks would
resemble rings on the disk, and the sector divisions would
look like pie-shaped wedges dividing the surface into 9,
15, 18, or 36 pieces, the number again depending on the
capacity of the disk. The following table shows the number
of tracks and sectors on floppy disks of standard sizes and
capacities.

STANDARD FLOPPY DISK FORMATS

Floppy Disk Size	Disk Capacity	Tracks per Side	Sectors per Track
5¼ inches	360 KB	40	9
5¼ inches	1.2 MB	80	15
3½ inches	720 KB	80	9
3½ inches	1.44 MB	80	18
3½ inches	2.88 MB	80	36

DISK-MANAGEMENT COMMANDS

The commands described in this chapter are those that affect entire disks. Each description shows the most common ways to use a command; use the DOS Help command to investigate more options if you need them. As described in the Introduction, all commands are shown in a general format, followed by examples that show how you would actually use them.

Format

Although you can't see the information stored on it, every disk you use is organized in a way that enables DOS to save information neatly and later retrieve that information accurately. This organization is not built into a disk; it is written there by DOS during the process called *formatting*. Formatting is needed only the first time you use a disk, but it *is* needed because DOS cannot use an unformatted disk. You can also recycle old disks by reformatting them.

For the most part, you will use the Format command to prepare floppy disks. A hard disk is formatted before DOS is installed and normally remains usable—without reformatting—for the rest of its working life. You cannot use Format on a network drive.

Caution: Reformatting, especially reformatting a hard disk, is not an action to be taken lightly. DOS does include an Unformat command that can undo an accidental format, but it cannot always guarantee total recovery. With previously used disks, use Format with care.

Perhaps the most important of the disk-related DOS commands, Format includes a number of switches that let you customize its operation. The most important switches are described here in separate sections.

To Perform a Simple Format

When you perform a simple format of a floppy disk, DOS formats the disk for the drive's standard capacity—1.2 MB in a 1.2-MB drive, 720 KB in a 720-KB drive, and so on. Use the Format command in the same way to prepare a hard disk, but remember: Format a hard disk *only if* you must.

Command form:

format *drive*:

☐ *drive* is the letter of the drive in which you want to
format the disk. You supply the drive letter, such as a,
b, or c. Be sure to include the colon.

Examples: If the current drive is C and you want to format
a disk in drive A, type

`C:\>`format a:

From drive A, the following command formats the disk
in drive B:

`A:\>`format b:

If you have one floppy disk drive and you type the preceding command, DOS uses the same drive alternately as
A and B, and it prompts you to exchange disks when
necessary.

In carrying out the format, DOS displays a number of
messages on the screen. The beginning message varies,
depending on whether you are formatting a hard disk, a
new floppy disk, or a previously used floppy disk. If you
specify a hard disk to format, DOS displays the following
warning (where *x* is the letter of the hard disk):

```
WARNING, ALL DATA ON NON-REMOVABLE DISK
DRIVE X: WILL BE LOST!
Proceed with Format (Y/N)?
```

Be sure you want to continue. If you do, type *Y* for *yes*
and press Enter. If you don't want to continue, type *N* and
press Enter; DOS cancels the Format command.

If you are formatting a floppy disk, DOS begins with a
message telling you to place the disk to be formatted in the
drive you specified (for this example, drive A):

```
Insert new diskette for drive A:
and press ENTER when ready...
```

When you're formatting a disk in a floppy drive, Format
always asks you to insert a disk and press Enter. This gives
you a chance to remove your system disk and insert a blank

disk. When you press Enter, DOS displays the following message while it determines whether the disk has been formatted before:

```
Checking existing disk format.
```

If the disk is new, this message is followed by a message similar to this:

```
Formatting 1.2M
```

If the disk is not new and is already formatted, you see

```
Saving UNFORMAT information.
Verifying 1.2M
```

In either case, once the format begins, you see a status report telling you *xx percent completed* (where *xx* will be a number). When the disk is formatted, the report becomes

```
Format complete.

Volume label (11 characters, ENTER for none)?
```

A volume label is a name you can assign to a disk. The label appears when DOS reports on a disk's contents: It's a useful way to identify a disk, but it's not essential. To assign a volume label, type a name (uppercase or lowercase) of up to 11 characters. You can include spaces, but certain other characters, such as the asterisk (*) and question mark (?), are not allowed. If you use a character DOS cannot accept, it responds *Invalid volume ID* and asks you to try again. Press Enter when you finish typing the label or if you don't want to assign one.

The formatting process then concludes with a report on the newly formatted disk. For a 1.2-MB disk, the report looks similar to this:

```
1213952 bytes total disk space
1213952 bytes available on disk

    512 bytes in each allocation unit
   2371 allocation units available on disk

Volume Serial Number is 0A33-0ADB

Format another (Y/N)?
```

The report tells you how much storage space is on the disk overall and how much is available for use. Consider 1 byte equivalent to one character. Sometimes DOS finds part of the disk unusable for storage. Don't be alarmed: DOS will not attempt to use unreliable portions of the disk. However, the report might include a line telling you there are *xxxx bytes in bad sectors* (where *xxxx* will be a number). If you see this message, remember that the storage capacity on that disk is reduced accordingly. If a large amount of disk space is unusable, consider discarding the disk.

The messages about allocation units and the volume serial number do not affect your use of DOS. The last line of this report asks if you want to format another disk. If you type *Y*, DOS starts the format process over again by asking you to insert a disk.

When you use other forms of the Format command, the messages are much the same. The remaining descriptions of Format assume you know what to expect during the formatting process.

To Format a Disk and Assign a Volume Label

DOS normally asks you for a volume label as part of the formatting procedure. You can skip this step by typing the volume label as part of your Format command.

Command form:

format *drive*: /v:*label*

☐ *drive* is the letter of the drive in which you want to format the disk.

☐ /v:*label* tells DOS you want to assign a volume label. For *label*, substitute a name of up to 11 characters, including spaces. You can use either uppercase or lowercase characters, but avoid unusual symbols (such as * and ?).

Example: To format the disk in drive A and assign it the volume label BLDG-PLAN, you would type

```
C:\> format a: /v:bldg-plan
```

The format would proceed as usual but with no pause to request a volume label.

To Format a Disk for Less than the Drive Capacity

There might be times when you want to format a floppy disk for less than your disk drive's standard capacity—a 360-KB disk in a 1.2-MB drive or a 720-KB disk in a 1.44-MB drive.

Command form:

format *drive*: /f:*size*

□ *drive* is the letter of the drive in which you want to format the disk.

□ /f:*size* tells DOS the disk capacity you want. For a 5¼-inch disk, you can use 360; for a 3½-inch disk, you can use 720 or 1.44.

□ /4 is a quick way to specify /f:360 (to format a 360-KB disk in a 1.2-MB drive).

Examples: Type either of the following to format a 360-KB disk in a 1.2-MB drive A:

C:\> `format a: /f:360`

or

C:\> `format a: /4`

Caution: A 360-KB disk formatted in a 1.2-MB drive cannot always be read correctly by a 360-KB drive. This form of the command is best used when the 360-KB disk you format will be used in another 1.2-MB drive.

To format a 720-KB disk in a 1.44-MB drive B, type

C:\> `format b: /f:720`

To Perform a Quick Format

If you want to reuse a previously formatted disk, you can perform a quick format, which takes much less time than either a normal or an unconditional format. You can do a quick format only on a previously formatted disk and only if you do not intend to change the disk's capacity (for example, by reformatting a 1.2-MB disk as a 360-KB disk instead).

During a quick format, DOS removes the record of file-names and storage locations that it keeps on the disk to help it find and retrieve files and locate available storage. DOS does not check the disk for unusable storage areas, as it does during a normal format, but it does maintain the disk's previous record of bad sectors.

Command form:

format *drive*: /q

☐ *drive* is the letter of the drive in which you want to format the disk.

☐ /q tells DOS you want it to do a quick format.

Example: To quick-format a previously formatted 1.2-MB disk in drive A, keeping the same disk capacity, type

```
C:\> format a: /q
```

When the formatting begins, DOS displays the message *Checking existing disk format*, followed by another, *Saving UNFORMAT information*. These messages are followed by

```
QuickFormatting 1.2M
```

(or whatever size disk you're formatting). Almost immediately, you then see

```
Format complete.
```

followed by a request for a volume label, a report on disk storage, and the message:

```
QuickFormat another (Y/N)?
```

Type *Y* to perform another quick format, *N* to return to the DOS prompt.

To Perform an Unconditional Format

An unconditional format is one in which DOS formats or reformats a disk completely: You cannot use the Unformat command (described later) to recover the information on a previously used floppy disk. If you perform an unconditional format on a previously used floppy disk, the information on that disk is permanently erased. Specify an unconditional format if you have trouble formatting a new disk, if you want DOS to check the disk for unusable space, or if you want DOS to erase the disk's prior contents as completely as it can.

Command form:

format *drive*: /u

☐ *drive* is the letter of the drive in which you want to format the disk.

☐ /u tells DOS to perform an unconditional format.

Examples: To perform an unconditional format on the disk in drive A, type

```
C:\> format a: /u
```

To perform an unconditional format on the disk in drive A, formatting a 5¼-inch disk for 360 KB, type

```
C:\> format a: /f:360 /u
```

To Format a Bootable Disk

Whenever you start DOS, your computer checks for certain DOS files on the disk from which you start the computer. One of those files, named COMMAND.COM, represents the part of DOS that accepts and carries out your commands. Two other files, which are important to DOS but not directly useful to you, are named MSDOS.SYS and IO.SYS. These files are normally hidden from view to protect them from accidental change or deletion.

One variation of the Format command transfers these three files (COMMAND.COM and the two hidden files) to the newly formatted disk, turning that disk into a *system* disk (one from which you can start DOS). Formatting a disk as a system disk can be useful if you want to create a floppy disk from which you can start both DOS and an application. You might also find this variation of Format helpful if you start customizing DOS to your computer's capabilities, as described in Chapters 7 and 8.

Command form:

format *drive*: /s

☐ *drive* is the letter of the drive containing the disk to receive the system files.

□ /s tells DOS to format the disk as a system disk.

Example: To format the floppy disk in drive A as a system disk, you type

```
C:\> format a: /s
```

DOS carries out the Format command as usual, but after you see the *Format complete* message, you notice some extra disk activity: DOS is transferring the system files to the newly formatted disk. When the process is complete, DOS displays

```
System transferred
```

followed by its usual request for a volume label, its report on disk storage (which includes the amount of storage occupied by the system files), and its message asking if you want to format another disk.

You can use the system disk as a startup disk, but it will not give you access to external DOS commands, including Format. A system disk, remember, is for starting DOS; it is not a replacement for DOS.

Volume and Label

A volume label is a name you can give to a disk to identify it. DOS requests a volume label when you format a disk, but you can view, assign, and change the volume label at other times as well. To do this, you use the Volume and Label commands. Although related, these commands have different functions:

■ Volume, which is abbreviated Vol, displays a disk's volume label and its serial number (which is assigned by DOS during formatting).

■ Label, which is not abbreviated, can create or change, as well as display, the volume label of a disk.

Both commands are simple in form and use.

Command form for Volume:

vol [*drive*:]

☐ *drive* is the letter of the drive that contains the disk for which you want to view the volume label. If you don't specify *drive*, the Volume command works on the disk in the current drive.

Example: To view the volume label for a disk named NEWSLETTER in drive A, type

```
C:\> vol a:
```

DOS displays something like this:

```
Volume in drive A is NEWSLETTER
Volume Serial Number is 0662-0CDD
```

Command form for Label:

label [*drive*:] [*label*]

☐ *drive* is the letter of the drive that contains the disk for which you want to view, create, or change the volume label.

☐ *label* is a new volume label you want to assign to the disk. Include this to create a new label or to change an existing one.

Example: To assign the volume label NEWSLETTER to the disk in drive A, type

```
C:\> label a: newsletter
```

DOS responds simply by displaying its prompt. To check on the new label, you can use the Volume command, or you can use the Label command by typing

```
C:\> label a:
```

DOS now responds with a display like this:

```
Volume in drive A is NEWSLETTER
Volume Serial Number is 0662-0CDD
Volume label (11 characters, ENTER for none)?
```

If you want to change the volume label, type the new label and press Enter. To change the label to CLIENT Z, for example, you can type

```
Volume label (11 characters, ENTER for none)? client z
```

If you want to either keep or delete the original volume label (NEWSLETTER in this example), press Enter when DOS prompts for a new volume label:

```
Volume label (11 characters, ENTER for none)?
```

DOS then displays one additional message:

```
Delete current volume label (Y/N)?
```

Type *Y* to delete the volume label; type *N* to keep it. DOS ends the command and displays its prompt.

Check Disk

The Check Disk command (typed *chkdsk*) allows you to check on both the condition of a disk and the amounts of total and available storage on it. As an extra benefit, Check Disk also tells you the amount of memory in your computer and the amount you currently have available for running applications. You can customize the command to have DOS report on the disk as a whole or to have DOS report on some or all of the files on the disk. You cannot use Check Disk on a network drive.

Command form:

chkdsk [*drive*:][*file*] /v /f

- □ *drive* is the letter of the drive that contains the disk you want to check. You can omit *drive* if you want to check the disk in the current drive. If you include a drive letter, be sure to type the following colon.

- □ *file* is the name of one or more files you want to check. If you don't know how to specify a group of files, refer to the description of filenames and wildcards in Chapter 4. Do not separate the drive letter and filename with a space.

- □ /v tells DOS to list the names of the files on the disk.

- □ /f tells DOS to correct storage errors if it finds them.

DOS stores long files by breaking them into smaller sections, each of which it saves in an appropriately sized portion of the disk. Sometimes these sections are laid out sequentially; at other times, especially on a much-used disk, the file is "fragmented," its sections distributed to physically separated portions of the disk. None of these details really matters to you because DOS records the location of each portion of each file you save, and it can retrieve the pieces in exactly the right order.

By using Check Disk with filenames, you can tell whether your files are fragmented. If your files are fragmented and you are concerned about it, you can "defragment" them either with a purchased disk-management program or (on floppy disks) by copying the files to a newly formatted disk; for details, refer to the Copy command in Chapter 4.

Check Disk might also reveal that certain files are not stored as neatly as they ought to be, perhaps as a result of an application failure that forced you to restart your computer. The evidence of this untidiness is that sections of files, which DOS calls *allocation units,* have been "mislaid"—saved on disk but in such a way that DOS cannot find out which file they belong to. The condition sounds severe, but it isn't—allocation units are rarely mislaid. Even when they are mislaid, they seldom cause problems either for you or for your programs. Check Disk reports on such lost units and helps you save them if you so direct (by using the /f switch).

Examples: If the current drive is C and you want to check on the general condition of the hard disk, you can type either

```
C:\> chkdsk
```

or

```
C:\> chkdsk c:
```

Either command directs DOS to check drive C and produces a report like this:

```
Volume CALIBAN  created 08-30-1990 3:31p
Volume Serial Number is 1697-4D7D

  33462272 bytes total disk space
    143360 bytes in 7 hidden files
```

```
   73728 bytes in 29 directories
28579840 bytes in 931 user files
   10240 bytes in bad sectors
 4612096 bytes available on disk
    2048 bytes in each allocation unit
   16339 total allocation units on disk
    2252 available allocation units on disk

  655360 total bytes memory
  616016 bytes free
```

If the current drive is C and you want to check the disk in drive A, you type

`C:\>`chkdsk a:

If you want to check the file named MYNOVEL.DOC in drive A for fragmentation, you type

`C:\>`chkdsk a:mynovel.doc

If the file is fragmented, DOS tells you in the Check Disk report with a line like this:

`A:\MYNOVEL.DOC Contains 4 non-contiguous blocks`

To check the general condition of the disk in drive A and to list all the files on it, you type

`C:\>`chkdsk a: /v

Finally, if you sometimes see a message like the following when you run the Check Disk command, DOS is telling you that it found some allocation units that don't seem to belong to any files:

```
Errors found, F parameter not specified
Corrections will not be written to disk

    4 lost allocation units found in 1 chains.
    8192 bytes disk space would be freed
```

To correct the situation, type

`C:\>`chkdsk /f

DOS then gathers lost allocation units into a file in the root directory named FILE0000.CHK. (If you have more than

one such file, DOS names subsequent files in order:
FILE0001.CHK, FILE0002.CHK, and so on.) You can
then use your word processor or the MS-DOS Editor to
view the recovered information and determine whether you
want to save it.

Diskcopy

When you work with floppy disks, it's often convenient (or
necessary) to duplicate an application disk or a data disk.
You can use the Diskcopy command to create an exact
copy of the original disk. Diskcopy works only with floppy
disks, and because it makes a character-by-character duplicate, it works only with disks of the same size and capacity.

Command form:

diskcopy [*disk1*:] [*disk2*:] /v

☐ *disk1* is the letter of the drive that contains the disk
you want to copy. Don't forget to type the colon.

☐ *disk2* is the letter of the drive that contains the disk on
which you want to make the copy. Again, don't forget
the colon. If your computer has only one floppy disk
drive, you can use drive A for both *disk1* and *disk2*;
DOS will tell you when to switch disks by referring
to *disk1* as the *source* disk and *disk2* as the *target* disk.

☐ /v tells DOS to verify the copy. You seldom, if ever,
need this switch because Diskcopy is very reliable.
Use it, however, if you want to be certain that the
copy is accurate.

Remember that the Diskcopy command applies only to
floppy disks. If the current drive is your hard disk, you
must include both *disk1* and *disk2*, the *source* and *target*
disks, in your command. If the current drive is one of two
floppy disk drives, you need only specify *disk1*, the *source*
disk; DOS will copy from the drive you name to the current
drive.

Examples: If the current drive is your hard disk, C, and you
have one floppy disk drive, you can copy the disk in drive
A by typing the following command.

```
C:\> diskcopy a: a:
```

If the current drive is your only floppy disk drive, you can get the same result simply by typing

```
A:\> diskcopy
```

In either case, DOS will tell you when to insert the *source* and *target* disks in drive A. As the copy proceeds, you see status messages like this appear:

```
Copying 80 tracks
15 sectors per track, 2 side(s)
```

When the copy is complete, DOS displays

```
Copy another diskette (Y/N)?
```

Type *Y* or *N* as the situation demands.

If the current drive is A and you want to copy the disk in drive B, type

```
A:\> diskcopy b:
```

Disk Compare

You might, on occasion, want to know if two seemingly identical floppy disks are actual carbon copies of each other. One disk might, for example, be a copy of an application disk and you want to know if the copy is exact, to the point that every sector in every track on the duplicate matches the original. To run such a check, use the Disk Compare (typed *diskcomp*) command.

Command form:

diskcomp [*disk1*:] [*disk2*:]

□ *disk1* is the letter of the drive that contains the first disk you want to compare. Don't forget to type the colon after the drive letter.

□ *disk2* is the letter of the drive that contains the second disk you want to compare. Again, don't forget the colon. If your computer has one floppy disk drive,

you can use drive A for both *disk1* and *disk2*; DOS
will tell you when to switch disks by referring to
disk1 as the *FIRST diskette* and *disk2* as the *SECOND
diskette*.

Remember that the Disk Compare command applies
only to floppy disks. If the current drive is your hard disk,
you must include both *disk1* and *disk2* in your command. If
the current drive is one of two floppy disk drives, you can
simply specify either drive; DOS will treat that drive as the
one holding the *FIRST* disk.

Examples: If the current drive is your hard disk, C, and you
have one floppy disk drive, you can compare two floppy
disks by typing:

```
C:\> diskcomp a: a:
```

If the current drive is your only floppy disk drive, you can
simply type

```
A:\> diskcomp
```

In either case, DOS will tell you when to insert the *FIRST*
and *SECOND* disks in drive A. As the comparison proceeds, you see status messages like this appear:

```
Comparing 80 tracks
15 sectors per track, 2 side(s)
```

If DOS finds that the disks match exactly, it displays this
message at the end of the comparison:

```
Compare OK
Compare another diskette (Y/N)?
```

Type *Y* or *N* as the situation demands.

If DOS finds differences between the two disks, it displays a report like this for each difference it encounters
during the comparison:

```
Compare error on
side 1, track 6
```

If you've seen enough to be convinced the disks are different, you can halt the comparison by pressing Ctrl-Break.

Mirror

The Mirror command, like the Unformat command described next, appears in DOS for the first time in version 5. Originally a program developed by Central Point Software, Inc., Mirror handles three important functions on your computer:

■ It helps you guard against loss of programs and data by saving disk and file-storage information that you can use with the Unformat command to restore the contents of a disk after you mistakenly format it.

■ It saves information about deleted files so you can recover them, if necessary, with the Undelete command.

■ It saves special information called a *partition table* that DOS must be able to find in order to use your hard disk. If the partition table is damaged, the programs and data on your hard disk become inaccessible to DOS. By saving the partition information with Mirror, you give yourself a way to make the contents of your disk accessible again.

To avoid confusion, Mirror's several functions are described separately.

Some Background Information

To understand what Mirror does and when you would want to use it, you should know a little about how DOS stores information. Whenever DOS saves a file, it checks the disk to find an appropriate amount of available storage. On an empty disk, this is easy. If the disk is one on which you've saved, deleted, and resaved many files, the task becomes more difficult because usable space is no longer confined to pristine portions of the disk; it can appear anywhere you've deleted a file. In order to use storage space efficiently, DOS matches the files you save to the space it finds. It then breaks your files into segments and distributes the segments to available storage blocks.

Later on, however, the question becomes one of locating those segments and reconnecting them correctly. DOS handles this part of the task by maintaining a *file allocation table,* or *FAT,* on each disk. The FAT has a record of all the storage locations on the disk along with a set of "notes" that DOS uses, like clues in a treasure hunt, to find the pieces of a file, one after the other, in the correct order.

When you delete a file, DOS uses the FAT in a slightly different way, marking each storage location used by the file as available for use. As these locations are reused to store a new file, the clues in the FAT are lost, and DOS can no longer follow the chain of storage locations that held the deleted file.

Mirror offers an alternative set of file allocation records to the set DOS maintains. Of the two sets, the one kept by Mirror is generally more reliable and easier to use simply because Mirror is specifically designed to help you recover disks and files. If you do not use Mirror, or if you have not used it recently on a disk that you need to "rebuild," you can use the DOS storage records to try to recover lost data. Because DOS maintains these records primarily for its own purposes, however, bear in mind that recovery is less certain when you use DOS.

To Save Disk and File-Storage Information

One use of the Mirror command is to save disk and file-storage information that can help you unformat a disk. The first time you use the command for a particular disk, Mirror creates a file on that disk named MIRROR.FIL. If you mistakenly format the disk, the Unformat command can use the file-storage record in MIRROR.FIL to reconstruct the disk. Of course, the information in MIRROR.FIL is only as recent as your last use of the command. Any files you create or delete after you run Mirror are not reflected in MIRROR.FIL. To recover those files, you must tell Unformat to try the DOS records instead. For help in recovering a disk, refer to "Unformat," later in this chapter.

Command form:

mirror [*drive*:]

□ *drive* is the letter of the drive that contains the disk for which you want to record storage information. You don't have to include *drive* if you want to refer to

the current drive, and you can specify two or more
drives by separating them with spaces.

Examples: If the current drive is C, you can save file-
storage information about it by typing

```
C:\> mirror
```

Mirror responds

```
Creates an image of the system area.

Drive C being processed.

The MIRROR process was successful.
```

If the current drive is C, you can save file-storage information about it and about the disk in drive A by typing

```
C:\> mirror c: a:
```

To Save Information About Deleted Files

Another way to use the Mirror command is to save information that applies to undeleting files. Mirror starts a program called the *delete tracker*. The program sits in the
background in your computer's memory and does only one
thing: It records the name and storage locations of every
file you delete on every disk you specified in the Mirror
command. This information is saved on each disk in a file
named PCTRACKR.DEL. If you delete one or more files
and discover that you deleted them mistakenly, you can use
the Undelete command and the delete tracker to try to
restore the files.

Reminder: *Don't forget that DOS reuses the space occupied
by the files you delete. As soon as any part of a file's storage
is reassigned to another file, the information formerly stored
in that location is irretrievably lost. You cannot recover it,
with or without Mirror. What this means to you is that every
time you save a file, you decrease the chance of recovering
completely one or more of the files you deleted earlier. Undelete your files as soon as you realize that you need to
recover them. If you manage to undelete before saving any
other files, your chances of recovering the deleted information
intact are quite good.*

Command form:

mirror /t*drive* /u

☐ /t is the switch that starts the delete tracker.

☐ *drive* is the letter of the drive that contains the disk on which to track deleted files. Don't type a colon after the drive letter. You can start deletion tracking for two or more drives by separating the switch and drive-letter combinations with a space.

☐ /u is the switch that removes the delete tracker from memory. If you use /u and then delete one or more files, those deletions are not recorded by Mirror.

Examples: To start recording deletions for drives C and A, type the following command:

C:\> `mirror /tc /ta`

Mirror responds with the *Creates an image...* messages shown in the preceding section. These are immediately followed by

```
Deletion-tracking software being installed.

The following drives are supported:
Drive A - Default files saved.
Drive C - Default files saved.

Installation complete.
```

To remove the delete tracker from memory, type

C:\> `mirror /u`

Mirror displays

```
Deletion-tracking software removed from memory.
```

To Save Partition Information for a Hard Disk

When you use Mirror to save partition information for a hard disk, Mirror creates a file named PARTNSAV.FIL on a floppy disk—not your hard disk. If the disk partition were damaged enough for you to have to rebuild it, the file would be inaccessible if it were on the hard disk. To prepare the necessary floppy disk, format the disk with the command *format a: /s.* To be safe, you might want to save emergency backup copies of AUTOEXEC.BAT and, especially, CONFIG.SYS on the formatted disk. To make Unformat available from your emergency disk, you also need to copy the Unformat command, UNFORMAT.COM, to the disk. The following series of commands makes the necessary copies:

```
C:\> copy \autoexec.bat a:autoexec.sav
C:\> copy \config.sys a:config.sav
C:\>copy \dos\unformat.com a:
```

Command form:

mirror /partn

□ /partn is the switch that causes Mirror to save a copy of the partition table for your hard disk.

Example: To save a copy of the partition table for drive C, type the following command:

```
C:\> mirror /partn
```

Mirror responds as follows:

```
Disk Partition Table saver.

The partition information from your hard drive(s) has been read.

Next, the file PARTNSAV.FIL will be written to a floppy disk.  Please
insert a formatted diskette and type the name of the diskette drive.
What drive? A
```

Mirror proposes drive A; if you want to use a different floppy disk drive, type the drive letter. Otherwise, press Enter. When the table has been saved, Mirror reports

```
Successful.
```

Label the disk, put it in a safe place, and hope that you never have to use it. If the need arises because DOS cannot use your hard disk, you'll need to try the Unformat command, described next.

Unformat

The Unformat command is related to the Mirror command in that it can use the files created by Mirror to undo a disk format. You can use Unformat with both floppy disks and hard disks, although it's to be hoped you never mistakenly format a hard disk, especially one containing hundreds of important data files. The command cannot always reconstruct a disk completely, so the best safeguards continue to be careful handling of your disks, duplicating of valuable files on backup disks, and thoughtful formatting of disks you've previously used.

Unformat can use the Mirror file MIRROR.FIL to rebuild a disk, or it can use the disk-storage information recorded by DOS. It can rebuild a hard disk (but not a floppy disk) formatted unconditionally—with the /u switch of the Format command. Unformat can also rebuild a damaged partition table on a hard disk if it has access to another previously saved Mirror file, PARTNSAV.FIL, on a floppy disk.

To Unformat a Disk with MIRROR.FIL

You can use Unformat with MIRROR.FIL in either of two ways: to rebuild a disk or to check that MIRROR.FIL matches the system information on the disk.

Command form:

unformat *drive*: /j

□ *drive*: is the drive that contains the disk to unformat. You must include this information, even if you are unformatting the disk in the current drive.

□ /j is a switch that checks MIRROR.FIL against the information recorded by DOS. When you use /j, Mirror verifies the contents of the file but does not rebuild the disk.

Examples: To unformat a floppy disk in drive A, type

```
C:\> unformat a:
```

Mirror responds

```
Insert disk to rebuild in drive A
and press ENTER when ready.
```

If you press Enter, Mirror displays a long message telling you, among other things, that using Unformat can result in loss of data. It also displays the date and time of your last and next-to-last uses of Mirror and Format, both of which

save Unformat information, and it asks you to press *L* if
you want Unformat to rebuild the disk with the last (most
recently created) file or *P* if you want Unformat to use the
prior (next-to-last) file. In most instances, you'll want to
use the last file because it most closely reflects the state of
the disk at the time you formatted it.

Before the unformatting process begins, the command
offers you one last chance to confirm. If you type *Y*, the
disk drive hums into action, and a few seconds later Unformat announces

```
The system area of drive A has been rebuilt.
You may need to restart the system.
```

(You don't have to restart if, as is likely, you've rebuilt a
data disk you almost destroyed.)

If you want to check the Mirror file MIRROR.FIL
against the system information on the disk without rebuild-
ing the disk in drive A, type

```
C:\> unformat a: /j
```

Unformat displays a set of messages assuring you that no
changes will be made to the disk; then it checks the contents of MIRROR.FIL against the DOS information on
the disk and tells you whether the two sets of information
match. (If the contents of MIRROR.FIL do not match
the system information, you can still rebuild the disk with
MIRROR.FIL.)

To Unformat a Disk Without Using MIRROR.FIL

If you haven't used the Mirror command, you can unformat a disk by using the file-storage information that DOS
records. Unformat uses this method if MIRROR.FIL does
not exist, but you can also specify this type of unformatting
procedure if you prefer not to use MIRROR.FIL—perhaps
because its contents were not updated recently enough. You
can also use this command to see the names of all the files
Unformat can locate on the disk.

Command form:

unformat *drive:* /u /test

☐ *drive:* is the letter of the drive that contains the disk to
unformat. You must include the drive letter, followed
by a colon.

☐ /u tells Unformat not to use MIRROR.FIL, even if it
exists.

☐ /test tells Unformat not to use MIRROR.FIL, even if
it exists, and to show how it would rebuild the disk
without actually doing so.

Examples: To see how Unformat would rebuild the disk in
drive A, without actually unformatting it, type

```
C:\> unformat a: /test
```

To unformat the disk in drive A without using the information in MIRROR.FIL, type

```
C:\> unformat a: /u
```

Unformat warns that you might not recover all the information on the disk and then tells you that the unformatting
process occurs in two phases. The first is a search of the
disk, which is time-consuming but safe because nothing is
changed on the disk. The search begins with a message telling you to *press Y* if you want to continue. If you do, you
see the message *Searching disk...* followed by a line that
tells you what percentage of the search is complete and how
many files and subdirectories (groups of files) have been
found. If Unformat finds information to restore, it begins
the second phase and prompts you to confirm the recovery.

*Note to intermediate users: Because of the way DOS
saves files, you'll find that subdirectories in the main (root)
directory of an unformatted (reconstructed) disk emerge as
SUBDIR.1, SUBDIR.2, and so on. You can use the DOS Shell
to assign these directories their original names.*

To Rebuild the Partition Table on a Hard Disk

If the partition table on your hard disk is damaged, DOS
cannot use it at startup, so the information on the disk is effectively lost to you. A hard disk can be lost to use in other
ways, including an intermittent problem that occurs when
the computer's clock/calendar card needs a new battery.

(See your dealer about this.) If a damaged partition table is the problem, however, you can rebuild the table if you have already saved a copy of it on a floppy disk with the Mirror command, as described earlier.

Command form:

unformat /partn /l

□ /partn tells Unformat to rebuild the disk's partition table with the information from PARTNSAV.FIL on a floppy disk.

□ /l (lowercase L), typed in the same command as /partn, tells Unformat to display a disk's partition table but not to attempt to rebuild it.

Examples: To rebuild the partition table for drive C, using a copy of the table saved on the disk in drive A, type

`A:\> unformat /partn`

Notice that the current drive is drive A. Drive C cannot be the current drive because the hard drive would be inaccessible in this situation. You could start DOS only by using a startup disk in drive A.

To display the partition table for drive C, type

`C:\> unformat /partn /l`

Unformat responds with a report on the hard disk partition table, which describes the disk in terms of cylinders, heads, and sectors. Cylinders refer, roughly, to stacks of tracks—tracks in the same position on the top and bottom surfaces of each platter in the hard disk. Heads refer to the read/write heads. The information in the report, with the possible exception of the disk size, is of little practical use to you.

CHAPTER 4

Files

Whatever work you do with your computer, you use files. The files are of different types, depending on what they do. When you use DOS or an application, you use program files. Program files contain the working instructions for DOS and for your application programs. When you compose a letter or balance a budget, you use a data file. Data files contain the text, numbers, and graphics that make up the work you do with the computer. This chapter describes the following file-related DOS commands:

- Directory, for listing and finding files

- Rename, for changing the names of files

- Attribute, for assigning read-only and other attributes to files

- Type, for displaying the contents of files

- More, for pausing the display of files or long lists

- Copy, for copying files

- Delete, for deleting files

- Undelete, for recovering deleted files

NAMING FILES

DOS treats a file simply as a collection of information to be stored and retrieved as a unit. To distinguish one file from another, whether it is a program file or a data file, call for it by its *filename*. A DOS filename can be made up of two parts separated by a period (.). The first part of the name, which you can consider the filename proper, can have up to eight characters. The second part, the *extension*, is optional and can have up to three characters. Although the extension is optional, it is often significant in identifying the type of information a file contains—program files, for instance, have certain extensions that help DOS search for, find, and run your applications.

Assigning Filenames

Program files are already named, and you should not alter their names. You do, however, assign names to the data files you create. As a general practice, identify files as clearly as possible, within the limits DOS allows. Although these limits can seem restrictive at times, you'll eventually find that short filenames mean less clutter on the screen and less text to type and wade through in finding one file out of hundreds on a disk. For efficiency, develop some consistent naming practices. Spur-of-the-moment filenames can become completely inscrutable in a few short days.

The filename and extension cannot include certain keyboard characters that DOS uses for other purposes. Above all, remember not to use spaces. Other unusable characters are * , ? . \ / < > " and :. You can, however, use a hyphen or an underline character to separate words in a filename, and you can use numerals and such characters as #) (^ and $. The following filenames are perfectly valid: MEMO, BADCHECK.91, 8-4REPT.DOC. The filenames in the following table, however, are unacceptable for reasons that are commonly overlooked.

SOME INVALID DOS FILENAMES

Invalid Filename	Comment
EINSTEINRPT.DOC	Maximum length of filename proper is eight characters.
EXEC.MEMO	No extension is required, but the maximum length of an extension is three characters.
WHAT4.???	Numerals are valid in filenames; question marks are not.
CAT/DOG.OUR	Hyphens and underscores are acceptable ways to separate words; slashes (and spaces) are not valid.

If DOS cannot accept a character you try to use in a command that includes a filename, it balks and displays a message that varies with the situation. You might, for example, see *Invalid filename or file not found*, *File not found*, *Invalid switch*, or *Parameter format not correct*. If you get any of these messages, remember that an incorrect filename might be the reason DOS is refusing to carry out a command. Recheck or retype the command.

WILDCARDS

As files accumulate on disk, you can forget exactly how you spelled a filename. Sometimes, too, you'll want to copy, delete, or otherwise work with a group of related files. To help you on both counts, DOS recognizes two *wildcards,* special characters that can represent any other valid characters in a filename.

One wildcard, the question mark (?), can stand for any single character in a filename. You can use the question mark in specifying a filename, an extension, or both. Any of the file specifications in the following table would be valid:

FILE SPECIFICATIONS USING THE ? WILDCARD

File Specification	Meaning	Valid Matches
?A?.DOC	Any three-character filename with A as middle character and DOC as extension	HAT.DOC MAT.DOC RAM.DOC BAY.DOC
BOOKS.?OG	Any file named BOOKS with a three-character extension ending in OG	BOOKS.BOG BOOKS.SOG BOOKS.DOG
?OME.DO?	Any four-character filename ending in OME, with DO as first two characters of extension	HOME.DOC ROME.DOC SOME.DOS HOME.DOT

The second wildcard, the asterisk (*), is more elastic in that it can represent any number of other characters. You can use the asterisk as part of a filename, an extension, or both, alone or in combination with other characters—as shown in the table below.

Notice in particular the second entry in the table, *ME.DOC. Avoid using the asterisk in this way to refer to a group of filenames that begin with different characters but have a common ending. The result will not be what you intended because DOS stops ''reading'' when it encounters the asterisk and assumes you mean all filenames, rather than all filenames with the same ending.

FILE SPECIFICATIONS USING THE * WILDCARD

File Specification	Meaning	Valid Matches
ME*	When *listing* files, any filename starting with ME, regardless of length or extension	METHODS.DOC MEANS.ANY METAL
	With other file operations, such as copy or delete, any filename starting with ME, but only if it has no extension	MEENY MEASLES MECHANIC —but not— MEENY.MOE MEASLES.POX
*ME.DOC	Any filename with the extension DOC	SAME.DOC ROME.DOC —but also— FLEAS.DOC POETRY.DOC
ME*. (Note . in file specification)	Any filename starting with ME, of any length and with no extension	METHODS MEANS METAL
*.DOC	Any filename with the extension DOC	BIRDS.DOC A.DOC !!@#.DOC
BOOKS.*	Any file named BOOKS without extension or with extension of one or more characters	BOOKS BOOKS.12 BOOKS.OLD BOOKS.NEW
.	Any filename of any length and with any extension	Every file DOS can locate

PROGRAM FILES VS. DATA FILES

Program files are intricate sets of instructions—unreadable on the screen—that define the types of work you can do and the ways in which the computer can carry out that work. Unless you are a programmer or an advanced user, you should not delete or modify such files because doing so can make a program unusable. Program files typically have the extension COM or EXE. DOS searches for the COM and EXE extensions whenever you type the name of a program you want to run. Programs use other extensions too. DOS, for example, uses not only COM and EXE but HLP, SYS, VID, INI, and BAS. Avoid using these extensions in naming your own files.

Data files, unlike program files, contain the work you do and usually consist of readable characters, such as letters, numbers, and punctuation marks. When you create a data file with an application, the program usually assigns an extension to it. Although you can specify an extension of your own, programs generally search for their own extensions automatically, so you can save time and typing by accepting the ones your program uses.

You'll rarely use data files apart from applications, so you can leave the details of data-file organization to the applications themselves. You should, however, understand one fact about data files in relation to DOS: Some data files are totally readable when displayed on the screen; others contain specially coded—and unreadable—characters. If you try to use a DOS command named Type (described later) to display a coded data file, you see odd characters and often hear sporadic beeps from your computer. The characters and beeps are harmless but can surprise you.

Completely readable data files are known as *text* or *ASCII* files. ASCII is short for American Standard Code for Information Interchange, a standardized code for storing and transferring computer files. The ASCII code is universally recognized, and so its use ensures that data files can be moved from one program to another. Word processing programs usually offer you a file-save option that includes this plain text format. You can also use the DOS Type command to display text files on the screen.

FILES AND DIRECTORIES

When you work with documents without a computer, you group and store them in some logical order—addresses of friends in one book, bills in a desk drawer, deck plans in a folder. Your storage scheme might not be the same as someone else's, but that doesn't matter as long as your organization works.

As you accumulate files on a disk, especially on a hard disk, you can also store them in groups by creating file "folders" called *directories,* each of which you assign a name much as you do with files. The program files that make up a word processing program, for example, fall naturally into one directory; those for a spreadsheet program fall into another. Data files generally fall into their own directories, although the ways you can group them are many and varied. Some data files are related by type (letters vs. spreadsheets), others by subject or category (client A vs. client B, budgets vs. annual reports).

When you want to find, save, or otherwise work with a file, you often specify its directory name (called a *pathname*) as well as its filename. Depending on the situation and the command you're using, a complete *file specification* might include only a pathname, only a filename, or a combination of pathname and filename, perhaps with wildcards in the filename. Because this book is more reference than learning aid, the descriptions of DOS commands in this section include references to pathnames for those commands that accept them (despite the fact that directories are not fully explored until the next chapter). Where necessary, the descriptions tell you whether a file specification allows both pathnames and filenames, only pathnames, or only filenames.

FILE-MANAGEMENT COMMANDS

The ability to use file-related commands is a large part of using DOS effectively. The commands described here tell you how to list, display, and copy files and how to delete and, if necessary, undelete them.

Directory

The Directory command (abbreviated Dir) is one of the most frequently used of all DOS commands. You can use it in many ways to search a disk for one or more files. When DOS carries out a Directory command, it lists the names of all files that match the file specification you provide.

A typical directory listing looks like this:

```
Volume in drive C is MIRANDA
Volume Serial Number is 16E4-9EF7
Directory of C:\PROJECTS

.             <DIR>      09-16-91    1:48p
..            <DIR>      09-16-91    1:48p
FILE1                1024   9-18-91    3:06p
FILE2               32358   9-27-91   10:09a
FILE3    DOC            17 10-04-91    2:45p
FILE4    TXT         28160 11-11-91    8:34a
        6 file(s)         61559 bytes
                       24759552 bytes free
```

The first two lines of the listing identify the disk and its serial number. The *Directory of* line tells you the directory (group) in which the listed files are stored. The next two lines are, again, directory information. You can ignore these if you don't yet use directories.

The following lines, from FILE1 through FILE4.TXT, form the heart of the listing. Each of these lines tells you about one file on the disk. Using FILE4.TXT as an example, this is what the parts of the line mean:

■ FILE4 is the filename proper.

■ TXT is the extension. Note that no extension is shown for FILE1 and FILE2. DOS shows an extension only if one has been assigned.

■ 28160 is the size of the file in bytes. One byte is equivalent to one character.

■ 11-11-91 is the date the file was created. If you change a file and resave it, DOS updates this entry to show the date the file was changed.

■ 8:34a is the time the file was created. As with the date, DOS updates this entry if you change and resave a file.

The final two lines of the directory listing show the number of files (including the two entries labeled <DIR>), the total number of bytes occupied by those files, and (at the end) the number of bytes available for storage on the disk.

The Directory command is especially flexible in version 5 of DOS because it includes a number of options called *switches* that help you customize the output. The most important file-related switches are described in the following sections. One additional switch, /s, applies to directories and is described in Chapter 5.

A Simple Directory Listing

The simplest form of the Directory command lets you list all files or only those you specify by name. You can pause the display for a long list. If you have no need to customize your search beyond specifying a file or group of files and you are satisfied with a normal DOS directory listing, this form of the command is all you need.

Command form:

dir [*drive*:][*filespec*] /p

☐ *drive* is the name of the drive that contains the disk for which you want to see a directory listing. Be sure to include the colon. Omitting *drive* causes DOS to display the listing for the current drive and directory.

☐ *filespec* is the name of a file or group of files you want to list. If you type a complete filename, including any extension, DOS lists only that file. If you use wildcards, DOS lists all files that match the file specification. You can omit *filespec* and have DOS list all files regardless of name and extension. If you type both a drive and a filename, DOS searches that drive for the file or files you specify. If you include a pathname, DOS searches the specified directory.

☐ /p is the switch that causes DOS to pause after each screenful of a long directory listing. To continue to the next screenful, you press any key. If you include /p and the directory listing occupies only one screen, DOS ignores the switch.

Examples: To display a directory listing for drive C, the current drive, type

```
C:\> dir
```

To display a directory listing for drive A if C is the current drive, type

```
C:\> dir a:
```

To display the directory entry for a file named SHOWME.DOC on the current drive, you would type

```
C:\> dir showme.doc
```

To display the directory entries for a set of files with the extension DOC on the disk in drive A, you would type

```
C:\> dir a:*.doc
```

To display a long directory listing, include the /p switch in your command. For example, if drive A contained a disk with 40 or 50 files on it, you could see the first screenful of entries by typing

```
C:\> dir a: /p
```

You could display the next screenful, at your leisure, by pressing any key.

Here is a more concrete example. DOS requires more than one screenful to display a complete list of its own operating system files. If you have a hard disk, these files are in a directory of their own, probably named DOS. To see a listing of these files, one screenful at a time, you would type

```
C:\> dir c:\dos /p
```

(If you try this and it doesn't work, the directory that contains your DOS files might have a different name. When you get to Chapter 5, you'll learn how to find it.)

Displaying a Directory Listing in Wide Format

As an alternative to the /p switch, you can choose to display a long directory listing by telling DOS to use a wide format. When you do this, DOS displays filenames in columns across the screen, omitting file sizes, dates, and times to produce a more compact display. The wide format is especially useful when you want to scan a disk or directory to see what it contains without cluttering the screen with file information you don't care to see.

Command form:

dir [*drive*:][*filespec*] /w

☐ *drive* and *filespec* are as described for the preceding form of the DIR command. There's little point in specifying a single filename with the wide format, but you can include wildcards in *filespec* to list numerous related files, such as all files with the extension DOC on a disk full of data documents.

☐ /w is the switch that produces a wide directory listing.

Examples: To call for a wide listing of files for the current drive, type

```
C:\> dir /w
```

To call for a wide listing of all files with the DOC extension on the disk in drive A, you would type

```
C:\> dir a:*.doc /w
```

To call for a wide listing of all files with the extension COM in a DOS directory on drive C, you would type

```
C:\> dir c:\dos\*.com /w
```

Sorting a Listing

Version 5 of DOS lets you sort a directory listing in a number of ways, several of them based on information (such as file size) that normally appears as part of a directory listing. The /o switch described here lets you choose the order in which files are listed. You can sort files by name (as in a usual directory listing), by extension, by size, or by date and time; or you can group directories separate from files.

Command form:

dir [*drive*:][*filespec*] /o[:]*sort-type*

□ *drive* and *filespec* are as described earlier. Because you are sorting by category, you're unlikely to specify a single filename, but a filename containing wildcards can be useful.

□ /o[:]*sort-type* tells DOS the type of sort you want. You must type /o, but the colon is optional. You can specify any of the following for *sort-type*:

Sort Type	Resulting Order
N	Alphabetic by filename (A to Z)
E	Alphabetic by extension (A to Z); useful in grouping files by type
S	By size, smallest to largest
D	By date, earliest to latest, and within dates, by time
G	With directories listed first; very useful on a crowded hard disk

You can also sort in reverse order (Z to A, largest to smallest, latest to earliest, or with directories listed last) by typing a hyphen (-) before *sort-type*.

Examples: To sort files on the current drive by extension, A to Z, type

`C:\> dir /o:e`

or, omitting the optional colon,

`C:\> dir /oe`

To sort the files on the disk in drive A by size, smallest to largest, type

`C:\> dir a: /o:s`

To sort the files with the extension DOC on the current drive, listing them in reverse order by size, largest to smallest, you would type

`C:\> dir *.doc /o:-s`

To sort all files with the extension DOC on the disk in drive B, listing them by date, you would type

`C:\> dir b:*.doc /o:d`

To group directories and files on the current drive separately, listing directories first, the command would be:

```
C:\> dir /o:g
```

Displaying Files by Attribute

In addition to size, date, and time, DOS also keeps track of certain file characteristics, called *attributes,* that affect the way a file is treated. DOS recognizes five attributes: D for a *directory;* H for a *hidden* file, one that DOS normally does not include in a directory listing; S for a *system* file, generally a program file that governs the way your computer operates; R for a *read-only* file, one that you can see but not change; and A for a file's *archive* status, an indicator of whether a file has been changed since it was last backed up to a different disk.

Command form:

dir [*drive*:][*filespec*] /a[:]*attribute*

☐ *drive* and *filespec* are as already described. You can use wildcards to specify a group of files.

☐ /a[:]*attribute* tells DOS to display directory entries for files with the attribute you specify. The colon is optional, but you must specify *attribute* as D, H, S, R, or A, as described above. You can also display entries for files that *do not* have a specified attribute by typing a hyphen (-) before *attribute*.

Examples: To see a listing of all directories in the current directory on drive C, type

```
C:\> dir /a:d
```

To display a listing of all files on the disk in drive B that have the read-only attribute, type

```
C:\> dir b: /a:r
```

To display a listing of files on drive C that have the hidden attribute, type

```
C:\> dir /a:h
```

To display a listing of files on the disk in drive B that are not directories, type

```
C:\> dir b: /a:-d
```

Rename

The Rename command, abbreviated Ren, allows you to change the names of one or more files, as long as you do not try to move the file or files to a new disk or a new directory by specifying either as part of the new name. You can use wildcards in the file specification, but if you do, be certain you know what filenames will be affected. You can do a quick check by first using the Directory command to see the filenames DOS displays to match the wildcard specification. If you see no surprises, you can then use the Rename command to change the filenames.

Command form:

ren [*drive:*]*name1 name2*

- □ *drive* is the drive that contains the disk with the file or files you want to rename.

- □ *name1* is the name of the file to be renamed. You can include a pathname, and you can use wildcards.

- □ *name2* is the name you want to assign in place of *name1*. You cannot specify a drive letter or directory with *name2* because specifying either component would describe a new location for the file rather than simply a new name. If you use wildcards in *name1*, be sure that *name2* is specific enough that no new filenames (including extension) would be identical. DOS does not let you duplicate a filename in the same directory.

Examples: To rename a file on the disk in drive A, changing its name from LETTERS.DOC to NUMBERS.NUM, you would type

```
C:\> ren a:letters.doc numbers.num
```

To rename a set of files named SAMPLE1, SAMPLE2, SAMPLE3, and SAMPLE4 so that they acquire the new names MYFILE1, MYFILE2, MYFILE3, and MYFILE4, you would type

```
C:\> ren sample? myfile?
```

Attribute

Recall that the Directory command lets you search for files that have specific attributes. The Attribute command, abbreviated Attrib, allows you to assign desired attributes to your files. You can use the Attribute command to hide files from casual view, protect program files and sensitive documents from change, or (less often) indicate whether a file has been changed. You cannot assign or change the attribute that identifies a directory; only DOS (or a programmer) can do that.

The Attribute command is particularly useful in protecting files from change. If you use it to hide files, they don't appear in normal directory listings. Remember, however, that the Directory command can also search specifically for hidden files; this attribute is useful in reducing screen clutter, but it is not a true security measure.

Command form:

attrib [±*attribute*][*drive*:]*filespec* [/s]

- □ + turns on an attribute; − turns off an attribute. For *attribute*, specify one of the following: R for read-only, to protect a file from change; A for archive, to indicate whether a file has been changed since it was backed up to another disk; H for hidden, to keep a file from casual view.

- □ *drive* and *filespec* specify the drive and files for which you want to turn an attribute on or off. You can include a pathname if needed.

- □ /s is a switch that extends the command, telling DOS to process files in all directories within the current directory, instead of the current directory alone, as it would otherwise do.

Examples: To assign the read-only attribute to all files in your DOS directory, type

```
C:\> attrib +r c:\dos\*.*
```

To assign the hidden attribute to a file with the name PERSONAL.TXT, you would type

```
C:\> attrib +h personal.txt
```

Once hidden, PERSONAL.TXT would not appear in a directory listing, nor would DOS include it in the part of the listing that shows the number of files and the number of bytes of storage they occupy.

To remove the hidden attribute from PERSONAL.TXT, you would type

```
C:\> attrib -h personal.txt
```

Type

The Type command instructs DOS to display the contents of a file. This is a useful command when you want to scan a data file to see what it contains without having to start the application with which you created it. Bear in mind, however, that a file containing codes inserted by an application might be partly or completely unreadable.

Command form:

type [*drive:*]*filespec*

☐ *drive* is the letter of the drive that contains the disk with the file you want to display. If you omit a drive letter, DOS searches the current drive for the file.

☐ *filespec* is the name of the file to display. You can specify only one file at a time. You can include a pathname, but using wildcards causes DOS to respond *Invalid filename or file not found.*

If a file you want to display is too long for a single screen, you can use the More command, described next, to stop the display after each screenful.

Examples: To display a text file named NEWWAVE on the current drive, you would type

```
C:\> type newwave
```

To display a text file named GRTWHITE.TXT on the disk in drive A, you would type

```
C:\> type a:grtwhite.txt
```

More

The More command tells DOS to stop a long display after each screenful and wait until you press a key to indicate that you want to continue. This command is useful when you're displaying a long file with the Type command. It's also a good alternative to the /p switch that is available with the Directory command.

Command form:

command ¦ more

☐ *command* is a DOS command such as Dir or Type.

☐ ¦ more tells DOS to stop after each screenful and wait for the next keypress. Both the broken bar (¦) and the word *more* are required.

Examples: To display a long directory listing, such as that for your DOS directory, one screenful at a time, you would type the following:

```
C:\> dir c:\dos ¦ more
```

To display a long document named NOTES.TXT on the disk in drive A, stopping after each screenful, type

```
C:\> type a:notes.txt ¦ more
```

An alternative way to type the command when displaying a file (again using NOTES.TXT as a sample filename) is

```
C:\> more < a:notes.txt
```

This form of the command tells DOS to activate the More command and use it with the file named NOTES.TXT on drive A. You don't have to remember this use of More unless you prefer it.

Copy

One of the operations you perform most frequently with files is to copy them, usually from one disk to another or from one directory to another. There are many reasons for copying files: to transfer a working copy of a file (for portability) from your hard disk to a floppy disk, to duplicate a file for someone else to see, or to store a file on a floppy disk before deleting it from your hard disk. The Copy command does all this and more—it can also combine files, and, as shown in the short exercise on creating a sample file, it can copy from a device, such as the keyboard, to another device, such as a disk. The Copy command, like a handful of other DOS features, is essential to DOS and has been a part of it since DOS was released in 1981.

Notice that Copy *duplicates* a file, which is not the same as *moving* it; that is, Copy creates an identical file but does not alter or remove the original. If you want to move files from place to place, you can copy them to a new location and then delete the originals or you can use the DOS Shell, described in Chapter 9, to do the job.

*A **warning about Copy**: This command is easy to use and a snap to carry out, but you must remember that DOS does not allow duplicate filenames to exist in the same directory. When you use the Copy command, you tell DOS both the file to copy and the location to which you want to copy it. There's no problem in specifying the file to copy; if it doesn't exist, DOS tells you so. But if a file with the same name already exists on the destination disk, DOS overwrites the original file with the incoming copy—and you cannot undo the process.*

Most DOS users can relate incidents in which they have overwritten valuable files, so when you use the Copy command, remember that DOS assumes you know what you're doing. If you're in doubt, use the Directory command first, to check on whether a file (or files if you use wildcards) already exists at the location to which you want the copy to go. If DOS responds File not found *to the Directory command, you can use Copy without any worries about overwriting a valuable file.*

Copying to Duplicate a File

The most common use of the Copy command is to copy one or more files from one disk or directory to another. Variations of this procedure are described in the following sections.

Command form:

copy *source* [*destination*]

□   *source* includes the drive and file specification of the file or files you want to copy. You can use wildcards and can also include a pathname as part of *source*.

□   *destination* includes the drive and file specification of the place to which you want to copy the file or files. You can use a pathname, and you can use wildcards to alter the names of the files as part of the copy process, but keep in mind the possibility of overwriting existing files. You can omit *destination* if you want to copy to the current drive and directory.

Examples: To copy a file named BLOSSOM.BLU from the current drive, C, to the disk in drive A, you would type

```
C:\> copy blossom.blu a:
```

Note the colon in *a:*. If you were to omit the colon, DOS would copy the file to a new file named A on drive C.

   To copy the same file from drive A to the current drive, you would type

```
C:\> copy a:blossom.blu
```

You could omit the destination here because DOS assumes you mean the destination to be the current drive and directory.

   To copy a set of files with the extension DOC from the current drive to the disk in drive A, you would type

```
C:\> copy *.doc a:
```

   To copy all files named FINANCE, regardless of extension, from the directory DEPT on the current drive to the disk in drive A, you would type

```
C:\> copy dept\finance.* a:
```

Copying to or from a Device

You can use the Copy command to copy files to an output device, such as a printer, and from an input device, such as the keyboard. You'll undoubtedly use your applications for most such "copying," but the use of the Copy command described here is one you might find handy at odd times when you want to create a short file without starting an application. In this form of the Copy command, you copy characters from the keyboard into a file on disk.

Command form:

copy con [*drive:*]*filespec*

- ☐ con, short for *console,* is the DOS name for the keyboard. Typing *con* tells DOS where to find the characters to place in the file.

- ☐ *drive* and *filespec* are the drive and file in which you want to save the characters you type. A drive letter is optional, but you must include at least a filename. Remember that if you specify a filename that already exists, DOS replaces its original contents with the characters you type.

Example: To create a short file named MACBETH.TXT on the current drive by copying from the keyboard, type the following and press Enter:

```
C:\> copy con macbeth.txt
```

When you press Enter, DOS moves the cursor to a new line and waits for you to proceed. You can now type some text, pressing Enter to end each line:

```
When shall we three meet again,
in thunder, lightning, or in rain.
```

To tell DOS to save the file, press the key labeled F6. DOS acknowledges the end of the file by displaying ^Z, its internal code for "end of file." Press Enter again to complete the command; you then see

```
1 file(s) copied
```

If you use the Type command to display the file, you will see the text you typed.

Copying to Combine Files

You will seldom need to use DOS for combining files, but if the need arises, Copy can do this for you, too. When you combine files, you specify the files to copy either with wildcards or by separating them with a plus sign (+), and you specify the file to contain the copy as a single destination filename. To avoid accidentally overwriting an existing file, pay close attention to the ways in which you can use this form of Copy, as described below.

Command form:

copy *sources destination*

☐ *sources* includes the drive letter, if needed, and a file specification, using wildcards, of the files you want to combine. You can include pathnames.

☐ *destination* includes the drive letter, if needed, and the filename (including the pathname) of the file in which you want to combine files. You must include *destination* in this form of the Copy command.

If the destination file does not exist, DOS creates a new file for the contents of the source files. If the destination file does exist, DOS replaces its contents with those of the incoming files, and you lose the previous contents of the destination file. To be safe, either check for the destination filename with the Directory command before combining files, or copy the source files to a filename that you know does not exist. You can always rename the file later.

copy *source1+source2+...source*n [*destination*]

☐ *source1*, *source2*...*source*n represent the drive letter and file specification (including pathname) of each of the files you want to combine. Use this form of the command if the files you want to combine are on different disks or in different directories.

☐ + tells DOS to combine the source files.

☐ *destination* is the drive, pathname (if any), and filename of the file in which you want to combine files. Omit *destination* if you want DOS to add files to the file you list as *source1*. Include *destination* if you want to create a new file or overwrite an existing one.

Examples: Suppose you have three files. FILE1 contains the text *rain, rain, go away*; FILE2 contains *come again another day*; FILE3 contains *little children want to play*. To combine FILE1, FILE2, and FILE3 in a new file named FINAL, type

```
C:\> copy file* final
```

or

```
C:\> copy file1+file2+file3 final
```

If FINAL does not exist, DOS creates it. If FINAL does exist, DOS replaces its contents. In either case, the result is

```
rain, rain, go away
come again another day
little children want to play
```

If FINAL contains the text *nursery rhyme* and you want to add FILE1, FILE2, and FILE3 to it, type

```
C:\> copy final+file1+file2+file3
```

Because this command uses the plus sign and does not specify a separate destination filename, DOS first finds FINAL and then adds FILE1, FILE2, and FILE3 to it. The file into which DOS combines the other files is the first file you specify.

Delete

Like hangers in a closet, files tend to proliferate without your being aware of how many you're accumulating. This is particularly true on a hard disk because it can hold such vast amounts of data. In addition, many applications, such as word processors, make automatic backup copies of files you change, so some data files can actually end up taking about twice the storage you expect.

The Delete command helps you unclutter your disks and remove files you don't need. DOS (except in the DOS Shell) doesn't include a "Move" command, but you can use Delete with the Copy command to move files. Copy them where you want, and then delete them from the original location.

Delete is easy to use, perhaps too easy when you're distracted or in a hurry. Before you type or carry out a Delete command, especially one using wildcards that can affect many files, be sure you know what you're about to do. Delete can prompt for confirmation before deleting a file, and version 5 of DOS does include an Undelete command that can recover files; but a prompt is only as effective as your concentration is focused, and Undelete cannot always guarantee complete success.

Command form:

del [*drive*:]*filespec* /p

☐ *drive* and *filespec* are the drive letter and file specification (including the pathname) of the file or files you want to delete. You can use wildcards. If you specify all files (*.*), DOS automatically prompts for confirmation before carrying out the command. In all other instances, DOS does not prompt unless you use the /p switch.

☐ /p tells DOS to prompt for confirmation by displaying the name of the file it will delete, followed by the message *Delete (Y/N)?* Type *Y* to delete the file or *N* to cancel the command. If you use wildcards to specify a set of files and also use the /p switch, DOS displays its message and prompts for confirmation with each file that matches the file specification.

Examples: To delete a file named OLDNEWS.DOC on the current drive, C, you would type

```
C:\> del oldnews.doc
```

To delete the same file if it were on the disk in drive A, prompting for confirmation, you would type

```
C:\> del a:oldnews.doc /p
```

To delete from the current drive a set of files named YEARLAST.DOC, YEARPAST.TXT, YEARDONE.FIN, and YEARGONE.OLD—prompting for confirmation with each file—you would type

```
C:\> del year*.* /p
```

Undelete

No matter how careful you are in deleting files, it's almost inevitable that you'll accidentally delete a file you need. Before version 5 of DOS, you had to purchase a separate program to recover such a file. With version 5, you have the Undelete command.

Undelete is one of three related programs from Central Point Software, Inc. The others, Mirror and Unformat, are described in Chapter 3. All three are designed to help you manage disks and file storage. Unformat and Undelete work in partnership with Mirror, which keeps a ''master list'' of disk activities that the other two commands can use.

If you've used the Mirror command to start the deletion-tracking feature, Undelete can work with the file-deletion records kept by Mirror. If you have not used Mirror, or if you prefer not to, Undelete can also attempt to recover files by using the internal file-storage records kept by DOS. Of these two methods, using Undelete with Mirror is the more reliable.

Although Undelete can be invaluable in recovering lost information, it is not infallible, and you should not make a habit of carelessly deleting files on the assumption that Undelete can recover any you later find necessary. If you accidentally delete one or more files and realize your error immediately, your chances of recovering the information are very good. If, after you delete a file, you do a considerable amount of work involving a lot of disk activity, your chances of recovering the information in that file decrease each time DOS uses the disk.

Always bear in mind that DOS continually maneuvers blocks of information around on a disk, saving and resaving files—sometimes in the space formerly occupied by part or all of a deleted file. Once disk space is reused, the information it used to hold is lost. DOS cannot recover it, and neither can Mirror or Undelete.

Command form:

  undelete [*drive*:][*filespec*] /list /all /dt /dos

☐ *drive* and *filespec* represent the drive letter and file specification (including pathnames) of the file or files you want to undelete. If you omit *drive*, Undelete attempts to recover the specified files from the current drive and directory. If you omit *filespec*, Undelete assumes that you want to recover all deleted files in the specified drive or directory.

☐ /list is a switch that tells Undelete to list, without attempting to recover, all deleted files it can locate. When you use this switch, Undelete uses a single asterisk (*) to mark files that are partially recoverable and uses a double asterisk (**) to mark those that are totally unrecoverable.

☐ /all tells Undelete to recover all specified files without prompting for confirmation before recovering each one, as it would otherwise do. If you use the /all switch with the records kept by DOS instead of those kept by Mirror, Undelete replaces the first character of each recovered filename with # or another unique symbol. Use the DOS Rename command later to correct the filenames.

☐ /dt tells Undelete to use the deletion tracking file kept by Mirror. Undelete assumes this switch if a deletion-tracking file exists. During recovery, Undelete prompts for confirmation before recovering each file it finds.

☐ /dos tells Undelete to use the records kept by DOS, even if a deletion-tracking file exists. Try this switch if you deleted files after turning off deletion tracking with the /u switch of the Mirror command. If you use /dos, Undelete prompts for confirmation before recovery of each file and replaces the first character of each recovered filename with # or a similar character.

Examples: Suppose you have deleted the following files on drive C: SWANS.DOC, GEESE.DOC, OWLS.DOC, and CANARIES.DOC. You now want to recover as many of these files as you can.

To recover the files if you started deletion tracking before deleting the files, you would type

```
C:\> undelete *.doc
```

Undelete displays its usual lengthy opening messages telling you what it is doing. In this message, *clusters* refers to the blocks of characters DOS treats as separate units of storage; *MS-DOS directory* refers to the records kept by DOS.

```
Directory: C:\
File Specifications: *.DOC

    Deletion-tracking file contains    4 deleted files.
    Of those,    4 files have all clusters available,
                 0 files have some clusters available,
                 0 files have no clusters available.

    MS-DOS directory contains    4 deleted files.
    Of those,    4 files may be recovered.
```

If the deletion-tracking file exists and you are using it to recover files, Undelete displays a message acknowledging that fact and a report like the following for each recoverable file:

```
    CANARIES DOC       2  7-19-91  3:03p  ...A  Deleted: 7-19-91  3:04p
All of the clusters for this file are available. Undelete (Y/N)?
```

To undelete the file, type *Y*; to skip to the next (if any), type *N*. If the recovery is successful, Undelete displays *File successfully undeleted.*

To recover files without using the deletion-tracking file, you type

```
C:\> undelete *.doc /dos
```

After displaying its opening messages, Undelete displays *Using the MS-DOS directory*, followed by lines like this for each file it found:

```
?WANS    DOC       2  7-19-91  3:03p  ...A  Undelete (Y/N)?
```

If you type *Y* to recover the file, Undelete displays

```
Please type the first character for ?WANS    .DOC:
```

Undelete needs this information because DOS replaces the first character of the filename with a special code whenever it deletes a file. Type the first letter of the file-name, and if the recovery is successful, Undelete displays the message *File successfully undeleted*.

To list the deleted files without recovering them, type

```
C:\> undelete *.doc /list
```

Undelete displays something like this:

```
Directory: C:\
File Specifications: *.DOC

    Deletion-tracking file contains    4 deleted files.
    Of those,    4 files have all clusters available,
                 0 files have some clusters available,
                 0 files have no clusters available.

    MS-DOS directory contains    4 deleted files.
    Of those,    4 files may be recovered.

Using the deletion-tracking file.

        SWANS       DOC       2  7-19-91  3:03p  ...A  Deleted:  7-19-91  3:10p
        CANARIES DOC          2  7-19-91  3:03p  ...A  Deleted:  7-19-91  3:04p
        OWLS        DOC       2  7-19-91  3:03p  ...A  Deleted:  7-19-91  3:04p
        GEESE       DOC       2  7-19-91  3:03p  ...A  Deleted:  7-19-91  3:04p
```

If a file is partially recoverable, you see a line similar to the following:

```
* SWANS      DOC       2  7-19-91  3:03p  ...A  Deleted:  7-19-91  3:10p
```

If a file is not recoverable, you see a line similar to the following:

```
** SWANS     DOC       2  7-19-91  3:03p  ...A  Deleted:  7-19-91  3:10p
```

Finally, if you have no deletion-tracking file and want to recover all possible files without prompting, type

```
C:\> undelete *.doc /all
```

Undelete displays the message *Using the MS-DOS directory*, followed by entries like this:

```
SWANS      DOC       2  7-19-91  3:03p  ...A  Deleted:  7-19-91  3:10p
```

and *File successfully undeleted* for each recovered file.

CHAPTER 5

Directories

If you've been working your way through this book, you've
made some slight acquaintance with directories, often
referred to as *subdirectories*. In this chapter, you'll find out
exactly what they are and why you'll want to use them. If
you have a hard disk, directories will soon become essential to organizing your files. This chapter describes the following directory-related DOS commands:

- Make Directory, for creating directories

- Change Directory, for moving from one directory to
  another

- Remove Directory, for deleting unneeded directories

- Tree, for displaying your directories

- Directory (again), for searching through directories

- Xcopy, for copying selected directories and the files
  they contain

- Replace, for replacing files in, or adding files to,
  selected directories

- Backup and Restore, for archiving and unarchiving files

DIRECTORIES AND WHY YOU NEED THEM

If you were stocking a warehouse, you wouldn't haul prod-
ucts in and stack them wherever you felt like putting them.
Such a scheme would work at first, when you had only a
few items to worry about, but it would quickly become un-
wieldy as you added inventory. Eventually, you'd have to
search the entire warehouse to find one particular item.
The obvious answer is organization.

The same type of thinking applies to your computer disks, especially your hard disk if you have one, because it is capable of holding so much information. You'd organize a warehouse by dividing it and subdividing it with rooms, shelves, and perhaps bins on shelves.

Directories are to your disks what rooms, shelves, and bins are to a warehouse. When you organize your files in directories, you can place each of your applications in its own directory, and you can, if you want, divide that directory in any way you choose. Or you can group your applications and create dozens of other directories to hold your documents, subdividing the directories as you want and organizing them in any way that suits your needs.

THE STRUCTURE OF DIRECTORIES

All directories start from a common point, a top level called the *root directory,* and branch off to lower levels from that point. Because of this branching effect, DOS is known as having a *hierarchical* or *treelike* directory structure. The following illustration shows such a structure and demonstrates how each level would compare to the organization of the warehouse described above:

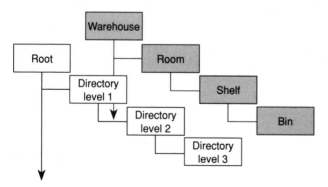

The Root Directory

DOS creates a root directory whenever it formats a disk. Because of its importance to DOS, the root directory is the one directory that you cannot create, modify, or delete. It is the home of all your directories and the subdirectories you create within them. The root directory can hold a large (but not unlimited) number of files and directories; in contrast, each directory you create within the root can hold all the files you care to stuff into it, up to the total capacity of your disk.

Unlike other directories, which you name in much the same way you name files, the root directory is identified by a single symbol, the backslash (\), which appears immediately after the letter and colon that identify a particular drive. Thus, for example, when DOS displays its prompt as C:\>, it is telling you that all commands will apply to the root directory of the disk in drive C. (The > character in the normal DOS prompt functions more or less as a "pointer" to the cursor.)

Directories

With the root directory of a disk as your starting point, you can begin to branch off to create directories. In general, you'll want to keep your applications in their own directories, and you'll probably want your data files in others. In fact, the installation program for an application often prompts you to copy the program files into a directory of their own. Applications often include a number of separate, interrelated files, so keeping a single application in its own directory makes sense, if only because the directory gives you a way of keeping those program files together and separate from other, possibly similar, files belonging to other programs.

Application directories, however, are a small concern. Once you've installed an application, it's there to stay until you delete it (which you can do—carefully—with the Delete command) or update it (usually helped along by the documentation or some type of installation feature that's part of the program package).

Document directories are a different story. Basically, you should consider creating a directory whenever the data file or files you want to save would be important enough (if they were on paper) to create a new file folder or a new division of your file cabinet. If you print all or most of your documents, you can even match your paper files to your directory structure, or vice versa, so you can work within the same structure on disk as on paper.

DIRECTORY NAMES

As already mentioned, directories have names similar to filenames. This isn't merely coincidental. To DOS, a directory is really just a file with a difference: Instead of holding data, a directory ''file'' holds the names of other directories and files. It's something like the difference between a novel and an address book. Both hold information, but of different types.

In naming a directory, you follow the same rules that apply to naming files: up to eight characters and a possible three-letter extension separated from the directory name by a period. And, as with filenames, certain characters, such as the space and the asterisk (*), are not valid. Thus, for example, NOTES, NOTES.MY, and MY_NOTES are all valid directory names, but NOTES.MINE and COURSE-NOTES are not.

PATHNAMES

To distinguish directory names from filenames, directories are often said to form a *path* to a filename, and a chain of one or more subdirectory names is considered a *pathname*. This term is appropriate because DOS literally follows the directory path whenever it searches for or saves a file.

Because you can create directories within directories, you separate one directory name from another with a backslash (\). An entire pathname, including the backslash separators, can have up to 63 characters—a formidable number of characters to type, let alone remember, and seldom (if ever) desirable.

When you create multiple directory levels, you can repeat directory names and filenames, but DOS won't let you duplicate a complete path and filename exactly. Here's an example. Suppose you create the directory PRIMATES within the root directory of drive C. Under PRIMATES, you then create the directory MONKEYS; and under MONKEYS, you create two directories, WILD and CAPTIVE. Under each of the lowest-level directories, you save two files, NOTES.DOC and REPORT.DOC. This is a diagram of your directory structure:

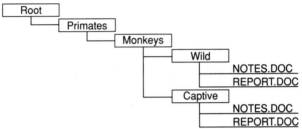

The following lines contain the paths to each of your files. You would type them in this way to specify the file locations to DOS.

```
C:\PRIMATES\MONKEYS\WILD\NOTES.DOC
C:\PRIMATES\MONKEYS\WILD\REPORT.DOC
C:\PRIMATES\MONKEYS\CAPTIVE\NOTES.DOC
C:\PRIMATES\MONKEYS\CAPTIVE\REPORT.DOC
```

To DOS, all four file specifications are valid—even though two filenames are duplicated—because no two paths, including the filename, are identical.

In typing DOS commands, you can include pathnames as part of the file specification in those commands that accept filenames, including the commands described in Chapters 1 through 4.

THE CURRENT DIRECTORY

You don't have to type a full pathname to identify every file in every file-related DOS command you use. Remember that your directory structure forms a hierarchy of many possible levels. Like the monkeys in the preceding example, you can clamber about your directory ''tree,'' jumping from one branch to another whenever you want by using the Change Directory command, described later.

Whenever you change to a different directory, that directory becomes what DOS identifies as the *current directory*. Subsequent commands apply to that directory unless you specify otherwise by including a different pathname in a command. When you want to identify a file in the current directory, all you do is type the name of the file. DOS assumes that the file is in the current directory.

While you're working, DOS keeps track of a current directory for every active drive on your computer and applies your commands accordingly. Thus, the current directory in drive C could be C:\PRIMATES\MONKEYS while the current directory in drive A is A:\CLOCKS. If you specify the file named HANDS.DOC for drive C, DOS searches for C:\PRIMATES\MONKEYS\HANDS.DOC; if you specify the same filename for drive A, DOS searches for A:\CLOCKS\HANDS.DOC.

DIRECTORY-MANAGEMENT COMMANDS

The following DOS commands show you the basics of creating directories, moving among them, and managing files within them. You'll use many of these commands routinely in managing data files.

The examples in each of the command descriptions show the current directory as part of the DOS prompt. This is done to help you envision the command's effect more clearly and also because the normal DOS prompt is designed to show directory names. If your prompt does not show directories, you can change it for the current session by typing *prompt pg*.

Chapter 7 shows you how to set your prompt as a permanent part of your startup routine. It also shows you how to use another command, named Path, to tell DOS the pathnames to your program files.

Make Directory

To tell DOS to create a new directory, use the Make Directory command, which you can abbreviate either Md or Mkdir. You can create a directory in the root or in any other directory on a disk, regardless of the current directory. The location of the new directory depends on the way in which you specify the path in your Make Directory command. The examples below show some common variations.

Command form:

md [*drive*:]*path*

☐ *drive* is the name of the drive that contains the disk on which you want to create the directory. If you omit *drive*, DOS creates the directory on the current drive.

☐ *path* is the pathname of the directory you want to create. If you don't specify a path, DOS creates the directory in the current directory.

Examples: Suppose the current directory is APPLES, on drive C. The following command creates the directory PIPPIN within APPLES:

`C:\APPLES>`md pippin

In the following command, note that the current directory is still APPLES. This command creates the directory ORANGES in the root directory of drive C:

`C:\APPLES>`md \oranges

The backslash before *oranges* tells DOS to create the directory in the root directory, not in the current directory.

Suppose the current directory on drive A were LETTUCE. From the directory APPLES on drive C, you could create the directory CARROTS in the root directory of the disk in drive A by typing

`C:\APPLES>`md a:\carrots

To create the directory ROMAINE in the directory LETTUCE on drive A, you would type

`C:\APPLES>`md a:\lettuce\romaine

Change Directory

The Change Directory command, abbreviated either Cd or Chdir, is your means of changing the current directory so that you can work in one directory and then switch to and work in another.

To reduce typing as you move around in your directory structure, you can use a form of shorthand consisting of two periods (..) to refer to the *parent* directory, which is the directory that contains the current directory. The examples below show how to use this notation.

Note: *If you use Change Directory to change the current directory on a drive other than the current drive, the change does not affect your current location. For example, from the root directory of drive C, you can type* cd a:\lettuce *to make LETTUCE the current directory of drive A; your DOS prompt will remain C:\>, however.*

Command form:

cd [*drive*:][*path*]

☐ *drive* is the name of the drive for which you want to change or display the current directory. If you omit *drive*, DOS assumes the current drive.

☐ *path* is the name of the path on *drive* to which you want to change. You can use the .. symbol for the parent directory as all or part of *path*. Specify *drive* but omit *path* if you just want to check on the current directory of the specified drive.

Examples: The examples below assume the directory structure in Figure 5-1.

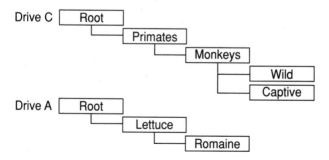

FIGURE 5-1. *Directory structures on a hard disk and a floppy disk.*

To begin, C:\PRIMATES\MONKEYS\WILD is the current directory. The DOS prompt following each example shows the new current directory.

To change to the parent (one level up) of the current directory, type

```
C:\PRIMATES\MONKEYS\WILD> cd ..
```

The DOS prompt then becomes

```
C:\PRIMATES\MONKEYS>
```

To change back to the directory WILD, type

```
C:\PRIMATES\MONKEYS> cd wild
```

To change to the directory C:\PRIMATES\MONKEYS\CAPTIVE, type

```
C:\PRIMATES\MONKEYS\WILD> cd ..\captive
```

meaning ''move up to the parent of the current directory, and then move down to the directory CAPTIVE.'' Or you could forgo the shorthand and type

```
C:\PRIMATES\MONKEYS\WILD> cd \primates\monkeys\captive
```

To change to the root directory of drive C, use the DOS symbol for the root (\) and type

```
C:\PRIMATES\MONKEYS\CAPTIVE> cd \
```

If the current directory on drive A were A:\LETTUCE, you could check the current directory from drive C by typing

```
C:\> cd a:
```

DOS would respond

```
A:\LETTUCE
```

Then, to change to the directory A:\LETTUCE\ROMAINE from drive C, you could type

```
C:\> cd a:romaine
```

Note that the specified path omits the current pathname on
A. You could also specify the complete path:

```
C:\> cd a:\lettuce\romaine
```

DOS changes the current directory on A, but because C is
the current drive, the DOS prompt remains *C:\>*.

Remove Directory

Directories can proliferate like files, though generally not
as rapidly. Some you'll want to eliminate because they're
old and either you don't need the files they contain or
you've copied the files to a floppy disk for safekeeping.
Other directories will simply be mistakes, or you'll decide
to merge the files from two directories and delete one
directory. For any of these jobs, you use the Remove Directory command, abbreviated Rd or Rmdir.

Command form:

rd [*drive*:]*path*

☐ *drive* is the drive that contains the disk with the directory you want to remove. If you omit *drive*, DOS
assumes the directory is on the current drive.

☐ *path* is the pathname of the directory to remove. If
you don't specify a full pathname, beginning with the
root directory, DOS assumes that the directory to remove is immediately below the current directory.

You cannot remove the current directory, nor can you
remove a directory if it contains files or other directories,
even empty ones. If you try, DOS responds *Invalid path, not
directory, or directory not empty.* Verify that the directory is
empty, and change to a different directory if necessary;
then try the command again.

Examples: Suppose drives A and C contain the directories
outlined in Figure 5-1. None of the directories contains
files. The current directory of C is C:\PRIMATES.
To remove C:\PRIMATES\MONKEYS\WILD, type

```
C:\PRIMATES> rd monkeys\wild
```

Because you did not specify the root directory (\), DOS assumes that both MONKEYS and WILD are in the PRI-MATES directory. If you had tried this command:

`C:\PRIMATES>`rd wild

You would see the *Invalid path...* message because DOS would search for and be unable to find WILD in the current directory. To use the *rd wild* command, you would first change to the MONKEYS directory, which is one level above WILD.

The current directory of the disk in drive A is the root. To remove both the LETTUCE and ROMAINE directories from the disk, you would deal with each separately. First you would type

`C:\PRIMATES>`rd a:\lettuce\romaine

and then

`C:\PRIMATES>`rd a:\lettuce

Tree

As you build a directory structure, you'll sometimes want to view all or part of it—perhaps to see where a new directory would fit best or to check on the way you organized a particular branch of the tree. You can see the organization of directories and files on any disk by starting the DOS Shell as described in Chapter 9, or you can view your directory structure directly from the DOS prompt by using the Tree command.

When you use the Tree command, DOS diagrams your directory structure by indenting directories under their parent directories and by using horizontal and vertical lines to connect related directories. A sample tree is shown in the examples below.

Command form:

tree [*drive*:][*path*] /f /a

☐ *drive* is the letter of the drive for which you want to see the directory structure. If you omit *drive*, DOS assumes the current drive.

□ *path* is the path to the part of the directory structure you want to see. Specifying a path indicates the directory level at which you want to start the tree; DOS displays the organization of all directories below that level. If you omit *path*, DOS starts with the current directory. To see a tree of the entire disk, either change to the root directory or specify the root as *path*.

□ /f is a switch that tells DOS to display both your directory structure and the names of the files in each directory. If you use this switch with the root directory of a full disk, especially a hard disk, the resulting tree can scroll through many screens of information, so you'll probably want to include the More command (as shown in one of the examples) to stop the display after each screenful.

□ /a is a switch that tells DOS to diagram the directory structure with plain ASCII characters (plus signs, hyphens, and slashes). This switch is helpful if you want to print the output of a Tree command but your printer does not produce the characters (known as *extended* characters or line-drawing characters) that DOS normally uses.

Examples: Suppose the disk in drive A contains some research you've done on forms of transportation. The current directory of drive A is the root. To see the directory tree, you would type

`C:\> tree a:`

DOS displays something like this:

```
Directory PATH listing for Volume TRANSPORT
Volume Serial Number is 066E-13DF
A:.
├──BOATS
└──PLANES
    ├──PROP
    │   └──BIPLANE
    └──JET
```

To see both the directory structure and any files on the disk, you would type

`C:\> tree a: /f`

To stop the display after each screenful, you would type

```
C:\> tree a:/f ¦ more
```

To see only the PLANES branch of the directory structure, you would type

```
C:\> tree a:\planes
```

and see

```
Directory PATH listing for Volume TRANSPORT
Volume Serial Number is 066E-13DF
A:PLANES
├───PROP
│   └───BIPLANE
└───JET
```

To print the entire directory structure, you would type

```
C:\> tree a: > prn
```

The > and the abbreviation PRN are described in Chapter 6. Briefly, they tell DOS to take the result of the Tree command and send it to your printer rather than to your monitor. If your printer can't accommodate extended characters, you would type

```
C:\> tree a: /a > prn
```

to tell DOS to use ASCII characters, which all printers can manage.

Directory: Searching Subdirectories

As files and directories multiply on a hard disk or on a high-capacity floppy disk, you can begin to have trouble finding a specific file. This is especially true when you create directories within other directories. Sometimes you'll want to determine whether a particular file exists on the disk; at other times, you'll want to know whether several related files exist in different directories. The Directory command can help.

Command form:

dir [*drive*:][*path*][*filename*] /s

□ *drive*, *path*, and *filename* are the letter of the drive you want to search, the path you want to search, and the file you want to find. You can use wildcards to search for a group of files. To search an entire disk, specify the root directory as *path*.

☐ /s is a switch that tells DOS to search the specified directory and all other directories it contains.

Examples: Suppose you have the directories on drive C outlined below:

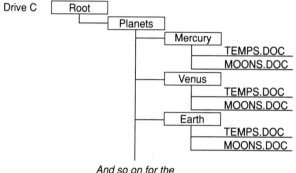

*And so on for the
other six planets*

To find and list all files related to planetary temperatures (TEMPS.DOC), you would type

`C:\>` `dir planets\temps.doc /s`

This tells DOS to search all directories of PLANETS for files named TEMPS.DOC.

To search for all files that have the extension DOC in all directories of PLANETS, you would type

`C:\>` `dir planets\*.doc /s`

To search all of drive C for a wayward file named MYTHS.DOC, you would type

`C:\>` `dir myths.doc /s`

KEEPING YOUR HARD DISK GOING

The commands described so far tell you how to create directories on your hard disk and work with the files in them. But effective use of a hard disk depends heavily on organization. Although organization is a personal matter, one sound approach is to keep your programs in individual directories and to create additional directories for your data files. Doing this allows you to categorize your data files in any way you like—by program type, by project, by date, whatever. Such an organization can cut down on the number of times you have to type pathnames but still leave you plenty of leeway to refine your directory structure as circumstances require.

Once created and full of files, directories are generally tedious to rearrange and reorganize. Although the DOS Shell can help with this, neither it nor DOS proper offers you any quick and easy ways to merge directories, figure out which files belong and which don't, or move a directory to a different branch of your directory tree. So when you're creating directories or planning new branches of your directory tree, think about how efficient they'll be, how you'll use them, and what you'll keep in them; then stick to your plan. For example, you could create an elaborate directory structure of 10 levels and categorize your files with scientific accuracy. Ask yourself, however, if you really want to expend the time and effort of typing 10-directory pathnames to change the current directory or to use a file. A little foresight can go a long way toward avoiding any ''Why did I do it this way'' and ''Where did I put it'' questions later on.

Because of its size, a hard disk can become both very important and very disorganized. To work with it comfortably, try to perform two tasks routinely: backup and cleanup.

Backups

The importance of a hard disk is measured in the amount and value of the information you trust to it. Although a hard disk is normally sturdy, uncomplaining, and extremely reliable, it is mechanical, and any mechanical device can have problems. If you've saved all your financial information or all your client data on your hard disk, you are risking a great deal if the disk suddenly becomes unusable. To minimize the impact of mechanical failure, you should regularly back up the files on your hard disk, saving them on floppy disks from which you can, if necessary, restore them intact.

Backing up a hard disk has the added benefit of copying old files you need to keep but seldom if ever use. By saving them on floppy disks (and deleting them from your hard disk), you make that much more room available for newer files. DOS includes two commands, Backup and Restore, that can copy your files onto floppy disks for safekeeping. You also have a choice of faster backup devices, such as tapes, and many off-the-shelf backup programs that can automate or speed the backup process.

Cleanups

Cleanups help you with disk organization. Without periodic cleanups, a hard disk can become full of useless or redundant files. Periodic housekeeping, boring though it might be, is really a necessity. Not only will cleanups help you organize your files and keep them readily available, they also help you make better use of your hard disk space by removing files that you no longer need to keep close at hand. As your data needs change, store your old files on floppy disks and clear them from your hard disk. If you no longer need a directory, remove it. Avoid clutter, and your work with both DOS and your computer will be easier.

The remainder of this part of the book describes commands that are exceptionally useful in maintaining order on a hard disk and protecting its contents.

Xcopy

The Copy command is useful for copying files and sets of files, but the Xcopy command is tailor-made for hard disks (or floppy disks on which you create directories) because it can copy both files and the directories that contain them. Use Copy for simple copying; use Xcopy when you want to duplicate a disk's directory structure on another disk.

Xcopy includes a number of switches; the most commonly used are described here. Type *help xcopy* at the DOS prompt to see the others.

Command form:

xcopy *source* [*destination*] /d:*date* /p /s /e /w

- ☐ *source* is the drive, path, and file specification of the file or files to copy. You can omit the pathname and filename, but you must specify a drive. You can use wildcards to specify a set of files.

- ☐ *destination* is the drive, path, and file specification of the destination for the file or files you copy. You can omit *destination* if you want to copy to the current drive or directory.

- ☐ /d:*date* copies files if their directory entries show a date equal to or later than the date you specify as *date*.

- ☐ /p prompts you to confirm before copying each file you specified in *source*.

- ☐ /s copies all directories (*s* for subdirectories) in *source* unless they're empty.

- ☐ /e is used with /s to copy all directories in *source*, even if they're empty. Use this switch to duplicate a directory structure exactly.

- ☐ /w causes Xcopy to wait until you press a key before beginning the copy.

Examples: Suppose the disk in drive A contains this directory structure:

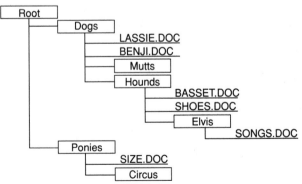

To duplicate the entire directory structure of the disk in drive A, including files and empty directories, in the current directory, ANIMALS, on drive C, you would type

`C:\ANIMALS>``xcopy a:\ /s /e`

To copy only the directories that contain files, you would type

`C:\ANIMALS>``xcopy a:\ /s`

To copy only the directories containing files dated 11-4-91 or later, you would type

`C:\ANIMALS>``xcopy a:\ /s /d:11-4-91`

To have Xcopy prompt before each copy, you would include the /p switch:

`C:\ANIMALS>``xcopy a:\ /s /p`

Xcopy would respond with a message like this:

`A:\DOGS\HOUNDS\ELVIS\SONGS.DOC (Y/N)?`

Type *Y* for *yes* or *N* for *no*.

Replace

The Replace command is a convenient way to copy files selectively. It can either replace files in one or more directories or add files to a directory. Replace helps you ensure that you don't mistakenly overwrite valuable files when you're copying directories from another disk.

Command form:

replace *source destination* /a /p /r /s /w /u

☐ *source* is the drive, path, and file specification of the file or files that you are copying to *destination*.

☐ *destination* is the drive and path that specify the location at which the files from *source* are to be copied. The *source* and *destination* directories do not have to have the same name. You can specify the same drive as part of *source* and *destination*.

□ /a adds files from the source disk that don't exist at
the destination. This switch does not copy files that
exist in both places.

□ /p causes Replace to prompt for confirmation before
copying each file.

□ /r replaces read-only files (in addition to normal, un-
protected files) at the destination.

□ /s extends the search for replaceable files to all directories (*s* for subdirectories) below the directory level
specified in the destination path. You cannot use /s
with the /a switch.

□ /w causes Replace to wait for you to press a key
before replacing files.

□ /u updates files at the destination if they are older
than the same files on *source*. You cannot use /u with
the /a switch.

Examples: Suppose you keep working copies of a set of
documents in a directory on drive C named WORKING.
The master disk in drive A contains the original files and
this directory structure:

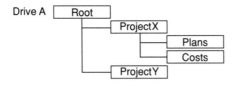

To replace all the files on drive A, regardless of the
directory, that also exist in C:\WORKING, you would type

```
C:\> replace working a: /s
```

To update only those files on drive A, regardless of the
directory, that are older than the equivalent files in
C:\WORKING, you would type

```
C:\> replace working a: /s /u
```

To replace all files with the extension DOC on drive A,
regardless of the directory, prompting before each replacement, you would type

```
C:\> replace working\*.doc a: /s /p
```

To add files from C:\WORKING to the directory
A:\PROJECTX\COSTS, you would type

```
C:\> replace working a:\projectx\costs /a
```

Backup and Restore

The DOS Backup and Restore commands work together to
copy files from one disk to another. Backup copies files,
leaving the original on the source disk. Restore returns
copied files to the disk and directory from which you
backed them up. You generally use Backup to archive old
or valuable files; you use Restore to return files to their
original locations. Backup and Restore work with files in a
special format, so you cannot use Backup to copy a file and
then use Copy or Xcopy to return it to the disk.

If you back up enough files to fill more than one disk,
Backup prompts you for new disks as it needs them. It numbers these disks, and the numbers are used in restoring
files, so be sure to label your backup disks correctly.

Backup and Restore include numerous switches that control the way they operate; only the most commonly used are
described here. To find out about the others, type *help
backup* or *help restore* at the DOS prompt.

Command form for Backup:

backup *source destination* /s /m /a /f [:*size*] /l[:*log*]

☐ *source* is the drive, path, and file specification of the
file or files to back up. You can use wildcards to back
up a particular set of files. You must specify *source*.

☐ *destination* is the drive to which you want to back up
the files. You must specify *destination*.

☐ /s extends the backup to files in directories (*s* for subdirectories) below the directory level you specify in
source.

☐ /m backs up files only if they have changed since the
last backup.

☐ /a adds backup files to the destination disk. If you
don't specify /a, Backup displays a warning and then
erases existing files on the destination disk.

□ /f [:*size*] formats the destination disk if it is not already formatted. Specify *size* if you want to format the disk for other than the normal capacity of the destination drive. Formatting takes time, so you might want to start with an ample supply of formatted disks.

□ /l[:*log*] tells Backup to create a log file listing the path and filename of each file it backs up. Unless you specify a different name as *log*, Backup names the log file BACKUP.LOG. The log file is always created in the root directory of the source drive. If you back up periodically, Backup adds new backup information to the log file each time you specify this switch.

Command form for Restore:

restore *source destination* /s /p /n /d

□ *source* is the drive containing the backup disk from which you want to restore files.

□ *destination* is the drive, path, and file specification of the file or files you want to restore. You must restore files to their original directories, under their original names. You can use wildcards to restore a set of files.

□ /s restores the files to all directories below the directory level you specify.

□ /p causes Restore to prompt before restoring a read-only file or a file that has changed since the last backup (overwriting the more recent file).

□ /n restores files only if they exist on the backup disk but not at the destination.

□ /d causes Restore to display the names of the files on the Backup disk that match the file specification. The /d switch does not by itself restore any files.

Examples: Assume that drive C has the directories shown on the following page. If the current directory is C:\, the command to back up all files from C:\PRIMATES and its directories to the disk in drive A would be

```
C:\> backup primates a: /s
```

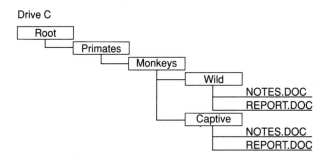

Drive C

The command to restore these files would be

```
C:\> restore a: primates\*.* /s
```

To back up all files with the extension DOC from
C:\PRIMATES\MONKEYS\WILD, creating a log file
named MONKS (no extension), you would type

```
C:\> backup primates\monkeys\wild\*.doc a: /l:monks
```

To see a list of the files backed up, you could display the
log file with the Type command or use the Restore
command:

```
C:\> restore a: primates\monkeys\wild\*.doc /d
```

Note that you must specify the pathnames and filenames of
the files you want displayed.

To back up only the DOC files in C:\PRIMATES-
\MONKEYS\WILD that have changed since your last
backup, adding them to the backup disk, you would type

```
C:\> backup primates\monkeys\wild\*.doc /a /m
```

To restore the DOC files on your backup disk that no
longer exist in C:\PRIMATES\MONKEYS\WILD, you
would type

```
C:\> restore a: primates\monkeys\wild*.doc /n
```

CHAPTER 6

DOS and Hardware

Most of the visible parts of DOS—the parts with which you interact directly—work with disks, files, and directories. As an operating system, however, DOS also deals with your computer hardware. Whenever you use DOS, it checks the keyboard for characters you type, displays your typing on the screen, and handles your disk drives. As a consequence, your applications can do the work they're meant to do without having to duplicate these fundamental and essential operations. If you tell it to, DOS can also work with hardware other than the keyboard, monitor, and computer unit. Its basic hardware-related commands are the subject of this chapter, which covers the following commands:

- Print, for printing one or more text files without having to start an application program

- Mode, for managing various hardware devices, including keyboard, screen, printer, and the communications device called a modem

In addition to these commands, you'll see how to use a feature called *redirection* to send directory listings, files, and other text to your printer.

DOS NAMES FOR HARDWARE

DOS is designed to check for and work with various types of hardware devices. To distinguish one from another, it assigns names to certain types of hardware. The section on copying files in Chapter 4 mentioned one hardware type,

CON. This is the name DOS assigns to your console—the keyboard and monitor. It uses only one name for both because neither can do the work of the other, and on most computer setups the keyboard and monitor together represent the primary devices for gathering input and providing output.

DOS also recognizes another major type of device known as a *port*. A port is a means other than the keyboard and monitor by which information can enter or leave your computer. On the machine itself, ports look like round or rectangular plugs and are usually lined up along the back of the computer unit. When you buy a computer, you're generally told the type and number of ports with which it's equipped. Most machines come with at least one *serial port,* and many computers also have one or more *parallel ports.* DOS assigns the name COM (for communications) to your serial ports, and it names your parallel ports LPT (for line printer). DOS allows up to four COM ports (which it identifies as COM1, COM2, COM3, and COM4) and up to three parallel ports (which it calls LPT1, LPT2, and LPT3). To confuse the issue a bit, DOS also sometimes refers to your first serial port (COM1) as AUX and your first parallel port (LPT1) as PRN.

Bits and Bytes, and How They Travel

When you type a letter of the alphabet, a numeral, or some other character, DOS does not work with a symbol in the shape of that character. It works with the character as a set of 8 *binary digits,* or *bits.* Each set of 8 bits is called a *byte.*

Binary digits belong to the binary number system, a means of representing numeric values with only two digits, 0 and 1. Because it uses only two digits, the binary number system is very comfortable for computers because the two digits can be represented by two states, on and off. In a group of eight (a byte), these digits can be combined in 256 different patterns. Each binary number, such as 10010101 or 01101101, can then be used as a code for a letter, a decimal numeral, a punctuation mark, and so on.

As your computer works with bytes of data, it moves them from place to place. Most visibly, it takes the code for a letter you type and turns it into a letter on the screen by moving the code, as a byte, through your computer. Not all information remains in the computer, though. Some characters travel out to your printer, and others arrive or depart through your modem. When you use one of these devices, DOS transmits or receives characters to or from the appropriate device through a port.

To guarantee that information is transferred properly, you tell DOS, either directly or by means of application software, what kind of device is attached to which port. And to do this, you must know whether the device you're using requires a serial port or a parallel port because not all information travels in the same way. A serial device, which must be attached to a serial port, sends and receives the 8 bits of a byte in sequence, one after the other. A parallel device, on the other hand, transfers the 8 bits of a byte all together, on separate, parallel wires. Some devices, such as printers, can be either serial or parallel; others, such as modems and mice, are serial only.

HARDWARE-MANAGEMENT COMMANDS

Most of the time, you'll find that you rely very little on DOS commands to deal with hardware. Applications and other programs can customize the screen and keyboard for you, and they'll even deal with DOS for you, to accomplish such operations as loading and saving files. When you print a document, your application, working alone or with an operating environment such as Windows, can take care of all the hardware details. If you want to connect with another computer, communications software can set up your modem to work properly. Still, it's good to know some hardware-related DOS commands. At some time you'll probably either want or need to use them.

Print

DOS includes a Print command that you can use for quick printing of text files. Print, unlike other DOS commands, is semi-independent and can work in the background while you go on to use DOS for other activities. This independence lets you place a group of files in a *queue,* lining them up for printing one after the other, and then go about other work with DOS.

Print is useful when you want to print files you create with DOS or save in plain text format with your word processor or text editor (such as the MS-DOS Editor). It is not as useful for printing other types of files because they can contain program-specific codes that wind up on your printout as odd symbols and characters. In addition, such printouts can contain unexpected line breaks or lines that are cut off at the right margin.

Print includes a number of switches, most of which you'll seldom, if ever, need; only the most commonly used are described here. To see a complete list of switches for Print, type *help print* at the DOS prompt.

Starting the Print Program

When you use Print, DOS loads the Print program into memory for the remainder of the session—until you turn off or restart your computer. When you load Print, you have some options about the way you want to use it. A few of the switches that control these options are described below.

Command form:

print /d:*device* /q:*queuesize*

□ /d:*device* names the port to which the printer you want to use is attached. If you have only one printer, you don't need this switch. You can specify *device* as LPT1, LPT2, or LPT3 for a parallel printer and COM1, COM2, COM3, or COM4 for a serial printer.

□ /q:*queuesize* tells DOS the maximum number of files it can place in a print queue. The normal print queue holds 10 files. You can specify *queuesize* as any value from 4 through 32.

Printing Files

To control the printing of text files, use the Print command with the file specifications and any switches that apply. If you are using Print for the first time since starting your computer, DOS prompts you for the device name and loads Print before it proceeds with printing.

Command form:

print [*drive*:][*path*]*filename* /c /t /p

- □ *drive*, *path*, and *filename* are the drive, path, and file specifications of the files you want to print. You can type several file specifications in the same command by separating them with spaces, and you can use wildcards to specify a set of files.

- □ /c tells DOS to cancel printing as described in the advisory note below.

- □ /t tells DOS to terminate the current print job and cancel the entire print queue.

- □ /p tells DOS to add to the print queue.

To see a list of files in the print queue, type *print*.

*A **word of advice**: When Print encounters a /c switch, it applies the switch to the filename that precedes it, plus all succeeding filenames until (or unless) it encounters a /p switch. The same rule applies to the /p switch. If you specify a number of filenames as part of a Print command, you can become confused if you also try to save time by adding some files to a print queue at the same time you cancel others. To avoid such complication, use /c in one Print command to cancel printing and use /p in a separate command to add files to the queue.*

Examples: Suppose you have the following set of plain text files in the root directory: TODAY.TXT, DONE.TXT, TOMORROW.TXT, and NEXTWEEK.TXT.

If you had only one printer, attached to LPT1, you would type the following command to print all of the files:

```
C:\> print *.txt
```

If this were your first Print command after starting the computer, DOS would first ask which printer to use:

```
Name of list device [PRN]:
```

[PRN] refers to the printer attached to LPT1 and is the printer DOS will use unless you request a different one. If PRN is fine, press Enter. To specify a different printer,

type the name of a different printer port, such as LPT2
or COM1. DOS then loads the Print program into memory
and tells you so by displaying

```
Resident part of PRINT installed
```

After these preliminaries, DOS begins to print; it tells
you the name of each file it prints by displaying a message
such as the following:

```
TODAY.TXT is currently being printed
```

To add a file named FORGOTIT.DOC to the print
queue, you would type

```
C:\> print /p forgotit.doc
```

To cancel printing of the file TOMORROW.TXT, type

```
C:\> print /c tomorrow.txt
```

DOS removes the file from the queue. If the file is already
being printed (instead of waiting in the queue), DOS prints
a message like the one that follows, below the last printed
line on the page:

```
File TOMORROW.TXT canceled by operator
```

To terminate printing and clear the print queue, type

```
C:\> print /t
```

DOS displays the message

```
PRINT queue is empty
```

and prints on the last page

```
All files canceled by operator
```

If you have more than one printer and want to tell DOS
to use the printer attached to LPT2, type the following as
your first Print command:

```
C:\> print /d:lpt2
```

You could then type the same Print commands shown in
the preceding examples to print files, add them to the print
queue, cancel printing, or clear the print queue.

Printing the Output of a Command

At times, it's useful to be able to produce a printed copy of the output of a DOS command, such as Directory, Type, Help, or Tree. You can do this with a feature of DOS called *output redirection*. Basically, output redirection enables you to send the results of a command somewhere other than their normal destination. This feature doesn't work with all DOS commands, but it can be handy with those that send their results to the screen.

Command form:

command > destination

- ☐ *command* is a DOS command that displays its output on the screen.

- ☐ *>* is the symbol that tells DOS to redirect output.

- ☐ *destination* is the place you want DOS to send the output. You can name a device, such as LPT1 (or PRN), or you can name a file on disk.

Examples: To send the directory listing of the disk in drive A to the printer attached to LPT1, type

```
C:\> dir a: > lpt1
```

or

```
C:\> dir a: > prn
```

If you're using DOS with floppy disks, a directory listing of the files on each of your working DOS disks can come in handy when you want to use an external DOS command, such as MIRROR.COM or UNDELETE.EXE, that is stored on a separate disk.

To save a directory listing for a floppy disk in drive A in a file named LISTS.TXT on your hard drive, you would type the following:

```
C:\> dir a: > lists.txt
```

To print a text file named PRINTME.TXT, you would type the following:

```
C:\> type printme.txt > prn
```

Similarly, to print the output of Help for the Unformat command, type

```
C:\> help unformat > prn
```

Mode

If any DOS command covers a multitude of functions, that command is Mode: It helps you set up (configure) the way your modem, keyboard, printer, and monitor work for the current DOS session. The following sections tell you how to use Mode to specify the number of lines displayed on your screen, set the rate at which your keyboard repeats, set up a serial port for communications or for use with a serial printer, and tell DOS to use a serial printer. You can also use Mode to check the status of devices attached to your system.

Note to the reader: *Mode also helps with a feature called code-page switching, which configures your keyboard, monitor, and printer for use with character sets, such as Portuguese and Romanian, that are not supported by the language for which your equipment is designed. This use of Mode is necessarily specialized and is not covered in this book. If you must customize DOS for multilingual use, contact your dealer or corporate resource, or obtain a book, such as* Running MS-DOS, *by Van Wolverton (Microsoft Press, 1991), that offers more extended DOS coverage.*

Mode: Controlling Your Display

Your display normally shows 25 lines of text with a maximum of 80 characters per line. You can use Mode to change both the number of characters per line and the number of lines on the screen.

To use the Mode command to control your display, your CONFIG.SYS file must contain a Device command in the form *device=c:\dos\ansi.sys*. If you try to change your display and DOS responds *ANSI.SYS must be installed to perform requested function*, the Device command is not in your CONFIG.SYS file. Chapter 7 tells you how to add this command and others like it to CONFIG.SYS.

Command form:

mode con [cols=*c*] [lines=*l*]

☐ con is the name DOS uses for the part of the computer that includes the monitor. You must include con to tell DOS which device you mean.

☐ cols=*c* tells DOS the number of characters per line of text. You can specify *c* as either 40, for large characters, or 80, for a usual display.

☐ lines=*l* tells DOS the number of lines to display on the screen. DOS can accept 25, 43, or 50 as a value for *l*, but you might not be able to use all three on your display. If DOS responds *Function not supported on this computer*, you cannot display the number of lines you specified.

Examples: To set your display to 40 characters per line, you would type

```
C:\> mode con cols=40
```

To set your display to 43 lines per screen, type

```
C:\> mode con lines=43
```

To set your display to 80 characters per line and 50 lines per screen, type

```
C:\> mode con cols=80 lines=50
```

Mode: Setting the Keyboard Rate

When you press a key and hold it down, your keyboard normally waits about half a second and then begins to repeat the character at the rate of about 20 characters a second. If you're a fast touch typist or often use repeat keystrokes (with such keys as the Spacebar and the Backspace key), you can use the Mode command (with most keyboards) to reduce the delay and increase the repeat rate.

Command form:

mode con rate=*r* delay=*d*

☐ con is the name DOS uses for the part of the computer that includes the keyboard. You must include con to tell DOS which device you mean.

☐ rate=*r* tells DOS how fast to repeat a character (after an initial delay) when you hold a key down. You can specify *r* as a value from 1 through 32; the higher the value, the faster your keys repeat.

☐ delay=*d* tells DOS how long a delay you want between the initial keypress and the first automatic repetition. You can specify *d* as 1 for 0.25 second, 2 for 0.5 second, 3 for 0.75 second, or 4 for 1 second.

Examples: To set keyboard repeat to its fastest speed and shortest delay, type

```
C:\>mode con rate=32 delay=1
```

To set keyboard repeat to its slowest speed and longest delay, type

```
C:\>mode con rate=1 delay=4
```

and prepare to fall asleep.

Mode: Setting Up a Serial Port

When you use a modem to connect your computer to another computer, or when you set up DOS to work with a serial printer, you must set up the serial port by defining certain settings. These settings are usually called *communications parameters* because they are most often used in establishing the speed and other ground rules that two computers use in transferring information. The standard communications parameters are the following:

■ baud: roughly, the speed of transmission, although usage is tending nowadays toward the more correct bits per second, or bps.

■ parity: the method used in checking for errors in transmitted information.

■ data bits: the number of bits used to make up one transmitted character (not always 8, even though 8 bits make up a normal byte).

■ stop bits: the number of bits that signal the end of a character (more precisely, the *time* needed to transmit those bits).

You'll probably use communications software for setting up your modem, but you can use the DOS Mode command as well. You'll also need this command for setting up a serial printer.

Command form:

mode com[*x*] [baud=*b*] [parity=*p*] [data=*d*] [stop=*s*]
[retry=*r*]

- [ ] com*x* is the name of the serial port. Depending on the number of serial ports on your computer, *x* can be 1, 2, 3, or 4. If you omit *x*, DOS applies your command to COM1.

- [ ] baud=*b* tells DOS the transmission speed to use. DOS accepts the following speeds for *b*: 110, 150, 300, 600, 1200, 2400, 4800, 9600, and 19200. You can type only the first two digits if you want—for example, 48 for 4800. Not all computers support 19200.

- [ ] parity=*p* tells DOS the type of error checking in use. DOS accepts the following for *p*: N for no parity, E for even parity, O for odd parity, M for mark, and S for space. DOS assumes E. (Even and odd parity are common methods that check characters by calculating values; the less widely used mark and space methods set a special bit to 1 or 0.)

- [ ] data=*d* tells DOS the number of bits per character. DOS accepts the following for *d*: 5, 6, 7, and 8. The most widely used are 7 and 8. If you don't specify this parameter, DOS uses 7. The values 5 and 6 are not supported on all computers.

- [ ] stop=*s* tells DOS the number of stop bits. DOS accepts the following for *s*: 1, 1.5, and 2. The default is 2 if baud = 110; otherwise, the default is 1. Not all computers support 1.5.

- [ ] retry=*r* is a parameter you might have to use in setting up a serial printer. It tells DOS what to do in the event the printer is busy or otherwise unable to accept transmitted data. DOS accepts the following for *r*: E, meaning report an error if the retry does not succeed; B, meaning report that the printer is busy; P (for "patience" perhaps), meaning continue trying; R,

meaning report "ready" if the retry does not succeed; and N, meaning no action (don't retry at all).
You can specify only one value for *r*. If you don't
specify a value for retry, DOS uses N. Don't use the
retry option with a network printer.

When you set these parameters, you don't have to worry
about deciding which values to use: The hardware largely
determines them for you. Check your hardware documentation, or (for a modem) check with the owner or manager of
the computer to which you're connecting.

Examples: To set up the serial port named COM1 for 2400
baud, no parity, 8 data bits, and 1 stop bit, type

```
C:\> mode com1 baud=2400 parity=n data=8 stop=1
```

To accept any of the values DOS assumes (the default
values), simply omit the corresponding parameters. For example, to set COM2 to 1200 baud and accept the default
values for parity, data bits, and stop bits, type

```
C:\> mode com2 baud=1200
```

Mode: Telling DOS to Use a Serial Printer

DOS sends printer output to one of the parallel ports it
recognizes: LPT1 (by default), LPT2, or LPT3. If you want
to send output to a serial printer instead, you must first set
up the serial port, as described in the preceding section,
and then tell DOS where to send the output. This is called
redirecting printer output. Again, you use the Mode
command.

Command form:

mode lpt*x*=com*y*

☐ lpt*x* is the name of the parallel port *from* which you
want to redirect output. You can specify *x* as 1, 2, or 3
for LPT1, LPT2, or LPT3.

☐ com*y* is the name of the serial port *to* which you want
to redirect output. You can specify *y* as 1, 2, 3, or 4
for COM1, COM2, COM3, or COM4.

To cancel redirection, retype the command but omit com*y*,
as shown in the second example on the next page.

Examples: To redirect output from the first parallel port (LPT1) to the first serial port (COM1), type

```
C:\> mode lpt1=com1
```

To cancel the redirection, type

```
C:\> mode lpt1
```

Mode: Checking Device Status

You can use the Mode command to see the status of the devices on your system—for example, to check whether a parallel port is redirected. You probably won't need it much unless you've used Mode to configure several devices, but if you need to use it, the command is simple.

Command form:

mode [*device*] /status

□ *device* is the name of the device you want to check on. It can be CON, LPT*x*, or COM*x*. You can omit *device* if you want to check on all devices.

□ /status (which can be abbreviated /sta) is the switch that requests a status check. You *must* use this switch when checking on a redirected printer because the command would otherwise become *mode lptx*, the command that cancels redirection. With other devices, you can omit the switch.

Examples: To check the status of the display, type

```
C:\> mode con
```

and see a report like this:

```
Status for device CON:
-----------------------
Columns=80
Lines=25

Code page operation not supported on this device
```

The code-page message indicates that this computer is not customized for other languages. Notice that the report does not include the keyboard repeat rate or delay values.

To check the status of LPT1, which you might have re-directed to a serial port, you would type

`C:\>`mode lpt1 /sta

To check on all devices, type

`C:\>`mode

The report for all devices is likely to occupy more than a single screen. To prevent the top of the report from scrolling out of view, you can send the output to More:

`C:\>`mode ¦ more

Press any key to see the next screenful of information, or hold down the Ctrl key and press Break to cancel the command.

CHAPTER 7

AUTOEXEC.BAT and CONFIG.SYS

Whenever you start your computer or restart it by pressing Ctrl-Alt-Delete, DOS goes through a standard startup procedure that concludes with a check for two files: AUTOEXEC.BAT and CONFIG.SYS (pronounced, by the way, "autoexec-dot-bat" and "config-dot-sis").

These two files are your means of customizing DOS in certain ways and preparing it to work with special devices and extra memory in your system. Most users are more familiar with AUTOEXEC.BAT, which contains the DOS commands you want to run each time you start your computer. CONFIG.SYS, which configures DOS for your computer, is less well known but frequently more significant. This chapter describes some of the commands you can use in these files to make DOS more responsive to your computer setup and your computing needs.

Note to the reader: If your computer is equipped with extended memory, you can include several commands in AUTOEXEC.BAT and CONFIG.SYS that will help you manage that memory efficiently. Because these commands apply only to certain, adequately equipped, computers, they are described in Chapter 8. Refer to that chapter if you have a computer with an 80386 or better microprocessor or if you have a computer with an 80286 microprocessor and more than 640 KB of memory.

DISPLAYING THE FILES

The DOS Setup program creates your AUTOEXEC.BAT and CONFIG.SYS files as part of installing DOS. The files are easy to locate: The only place DOS checks for them is the root directory of your startup drive. So if these files are in any other directory, even your DOS directory, they might as well not exist.

Unlike DOS program files, AUTOEXEC.BAT and CONFIG.SYS contain only text characters, so you can see their contents with the Type command. If you use DOS from a hard disk, type

```
C:\> type c:\autoexec.bat
```

and

```
C:\> type c:\config.sys
```

If you use DOS from floppy disks, verify that your startup disk is in drive A, and then substitute *a:* for *c:* in the preceding commands.

CHANGING FILES WITH THE EDITOR

A word of caution: If you experiment with AUTOEXEC.BAT and CONFIG.SYS, safeguard the original files by creating backup copies of them (AUTOEXEC.OK and CONFIG.OK, for example). Better still, format a floppy disk and copy the essential DOS system files to it with the format a: /s *command, and then copy your AUTOEXEC.BAT and CONFIG.SYS files to the floppy disk. Use this disk for startup to test your evolving AUTOEXEC.BAT and CONFIG.SYS files. Doing this keeps your original startup procedure secure until you're ready to change it permanently.*

You can use the part of DOS called the MS-DOS Editor to view and work with each file. The Editor works like a simple word processor in allowing you to enter, edit, save, and print files. Because it adds no special codes of its own to your file, the Editor is particularly useful when you want to work with plain text files that you'll use with DOS or with another program.

Starting the Editor

To start the Editor and load a file into memory, type *edit* followed by the name of the file you want to edit. To load AUTOEXEC.BAT from your hard disk, the command is

```
C:\> edit c:\autoexec.bat
```

And for CONFIG.SYS, the command is

```
C:\> edit c:\config.sys
```

The following illustration shows the MS-DOS Editor displaying a simple AUTOEXEC.BAT file:

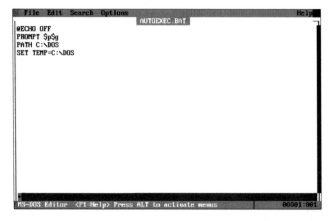

If you use an operating environment such as Microsoft Windows, the MS-DOS Editor has a familiar look because it too shows the screen's working area as a framed window with menu names across the top. You can open each menu (File, Edit, Search, Options, and Help) to reveal a group of related commands.

Using a Menu

If you have a mouse, you open a menu by moving the mouse pointer to the menu name and pressing (*clicking*) the left mouse button once. If you don't have a mouse, press the Alt key to activate the row of menu names (the *menu bar*). Each menu name changes to display one highlighted (white)

letter, and a black box appears around the File menu name. Choose a menu to display its commands: Press a direction key, if necessary, to move the black box to the appropriate menu name, and press Enter; or press the key on your keyboard that corresponds to the highlighted letter in the menu name. Use the same mouse or keyboard actions to choose commands from an open menu.

To open the File menu (shown below), move the mouse pointer to the word *File* and click the left mouse button, or press Alt and then press *F* or Enter.

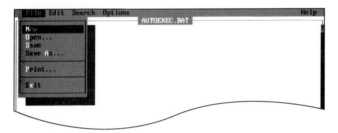

To close a menu, move the mouse pointer outside the menu and click the left mouse button, or press the Esc key.

Editing a File

To add text to a file, move the cursor to the location you want and type the new text. To move the cursor with the mouse, move the mouse pointer to the location you want and click the left button. With the keyboard, use the direction keys. You cannot position the cursor below the last line of text or paragraph mark in the file.

The MS-DOS Editor normally works in insert mode, so new characters are inserted at the position of the cursor, and existing characters are pushed to the right. To change characters within existing text, do either of the following:

■ Position the cursor and press the Insert key. This switches the Editor to overstrike mode, indicated on-screen when the cursor turns into a blinking rect-angle. Overstrike mode replaces existing characters with new ones you type. Press Insert again to turn off overstrike mode.

■ Position the cursor and press the Delete key once for each character you want to delete. The Delete key erases the character directly above the cursor. (You can also use the Backspace key to delete characters to the left of the cursor.)

Saving and Quitting

After you change a file, you must save it on disk if you want your changes to become a permanent part of the file. You can save a file at any time by opening the File menu and choosing the Save or Save As command:

■ Save saves a file on disk under its current name, so you use this command primarily to save changes to an existing file. If you change your AUTOEXEC.BAT or CONFIG.SYS file and want to save the changes, use the Save command.

■ Save As prompts you for a filename before saving, so you use it primarily to save a new file, to save an existing file under a new name, or to save an existing file under the same name but on a different disk.

To quit the Editor, choose the Exit command from the File menu. If you've been working on a file and have saved all changes on disk, your disk drive becomes active for a short time, and the Editor disappears. If you've been working on a file and haven't saved your changes, the Editor tells you so by displaying a dialog box that asks if you want to save the changes before quitting:

```
Loaded file is not saved. Save it now?

< Yes >    < No >    <Cancel>    < Help >
```

Yes, No, Cancel, and Help are buttons you ''press'' to indicate your choice. Click the mouse button on Yes or press the Enter key when Yes is highlighted if you want to save the changes to your file. To choose one of the other buttons, click on it, or press the Tab key to highlight your choice and then press Enter.

Learning More About the Editor

With the preceding instructions as a basis, you can begin your own exploration of the MS-DOS Editor. The Editor offers extensive online Help, which works well as a self-teaching aid and as a refresher for your memory. Help can give you guidance on using the keyboard, understanding commands, and even on using Help. When you want to browse the available information, use the Help menu.

If you have questions while using a command, press the F1 key, or if you're stumped by a dialog box that offers a Help button, choose the button. Both the F1 key and the Help button call up sections of Help that tell you what to do in the situation you're in.

AUTOEXEC.BAT

AUTOEXEC.BAT is an example of a batch file, a set of commands that DOS can carry out as a sequence instead of stopping after each command and waiting for you to type the next one, as it would normally do. The contents of an AUTOEXEC.BAT file can be as varied as the situations in which people use computers. The file can be as short as a few lines or as long as several screenfuls. To include a DOS command in your AUTOEXEC.BAT file, you type the command on a separate line in the file, exactly as you would type it at the DOS prompt.

Although most of the commands in an AUTOEXEC-.BAT file are DOS commands, AUTOEXEC.BAT is also used to load certain types of programs known as TSRs, for terminate and stay resident. These programs load into your computer's memory but stay out of the way until they are needed. Several DOS commands are TSRs. Among them are Print and Doskey, both of which you can start automatically by placing the command names in your AUTOEXEC.BAT file. If your computer has extended memory and an 80386 or better microprocessor, you can use AUTOEXEC.BAT to load many TSRs into the upper memory area, as described in Chapter 8.

COMMANDS FOR AUTOEXEC.BAT

A number of DOS commands are so commonly used in
AUTOEXEC.BAT files that people seldom use them directly from the DOS prompt. Three of those commands—
Path, Prompt, and Set—are described in this section. The
sample file following the descriptions shows a few ways
in which you can use these and other DOS commands in
AUTOEXEC.BAT.

Because DOS checks for an AUTOEXEC.BAT file only
at startup, you must restart your computer for any new or
changed commands to take effect.

Setting the Search Path

Left to itself, DOS searches only the current directory
when you type the name of a program to run, even if the
program is one of DOS's own external commands, such as
Format or Check Disk. On a hard disk, however, you'll
probably keep your DOS files in a separate directory, and
you'll also create additional directories to keep your applications neatly organized. To tell DOS where to look for
your programs—so that you can start an often-used application without first changing to the directory it occupies—
you use the Path command.

Path is a natural candidate for your AUTOEXEC.BAT
file; in fact, it's one of the first commands to appear in
practically every AUTOEXEC.BAT file. During installation, the DOS 5 Setup program creates a Path command in
your AUTOEXEC.BAT file. At some time, however, you'll
want to modify this command to add new directories or to
delete old, unused directories from the command.

Command form:

  path *directory*;[*directory*;]...[*directory*]

  □ *directory* is the drive and path of each directory you
    want DOS to search. You can specify a series of
    directories, as long as you separate complete
    pathnames with a semicolon.

When you specify a search path, DOS searches each directory in it for a program you want to run. If you type *path* alone, DOS displays the current search path. If you type *path ;* (note the semicolon), DOS deletes the current search path. You seldom, if ever, want to do this.

Examples: To set the search path to the directories C:\DOS, C:\UTILS (for utility programs), and C:\KIM\GAMES, you would add or modify the Path command in AUTOEXEC.BAT as follows:

```
path c:\dos;c:\utils;c:\kim\games
```

To add the directory C:\WORD to the search path, you would start the MS-DOS Editor, load AUTOEXEC.BAT, position the cursor at the end of the Path command, and edit the command as follows:

```
path c:\dos;c:\utils;c:\kim\games; c:\word
```

Or you could position the cursor after any semicolon in the line and add the new directory:

```
path c:\dos;c:\utils; c:\word; c:\kim\games
```

Either form would work.

To display the search path, type the Path command by itself (at the DOS prompt):

```
C:\> path
```

Setting the DOS Prompt

Throughout this book the DOS prompt has been shown as *C:\>*. This is the prompt Setup defines for you, and many people work happily with it because it is economical yet changes to display valuable information: the name of the current drive and directory. If you prefer a less succinct prompt or a friendlier one, you can customize it in many ways with the Prompt command.

To have a particular prompt appear each time you start your computer, place the Prompt command in your AUTO-EXEC.BAT file. You can type the command at the DOS prompt if you want to change the prompt only temporarily.

Command form:

prompt *definition*

☐ *definition* is a set of characters that defines the prompt to DOS. You can type a string of text, or you can tell DOS to display certain items by using one or more of the following codes, each of which begins with a dollar sign ($):

Code	Displays
$b	¦
$d	The current date
$e	An Escape character (used with a special display-control file named ANSI.SYS)
$g	>
$h	A backspace character (which erases the preceding character)
$l	<
$n	The current drive
$p	The current drive and directory
$q	=
$t	The current time
$v	The DOS version
$_	A new line (which forces the rest of the prompt onto the next line)
$$	$

If you type *prompt* by itself, DOS sets the prompt to a drive letter and a greater-than sign, like this: C>. Notice that this prompt does not show the current directory.

Examples: The Setup program defines the DOS prompt (in your AUTOEXEC.BAT file) as

```
prompt $p$g
```

The $p causes DOS to display the current drive and directory; $g causes it to display the greater-than symbol (>).

To display the current time on a separate line above the normal DOS prompt, type the following command at the DOS prompt or put it in AUTOEXEC.BAT (in place of the command DOS inserts for you):

```
prompt $t$_$p$g
```

Defined in this way, the prompt tells DOS to display the time ($t), go to a new line ($_), display the current drive and directory ($p), and end with a greater-than sign ($g).

To turn the prompt into the string of text *Next command?*, the command would be

```
prompt Next command?
```

Setting Environment Variables

The Set command defines certain variables that contain information about the environment in which DOS and other programs work. You can type the Set command at the DOS prompt to change a variable temporarily, but you more commonly put Set commands in AUTOEXEC.BAT to define routinely used environment variables each time you start your computer.

Setup defines certain environment variables for you during installation; one of these, named COMSPEC, gives the location of a part of DOS named COMMAND.COM. You can define other environment variables or change existing definitions with the Set command. Two environment variables, DIRCMD and TEMP, are especially useful to know about.

Command form:

set *variable=definition*

☐ *variable* is the name of the environment variable you want to define.

☐ *definition* is a description you want to assign to the environment variable.

To eliminate a variable you've defined, type the command without a definition. You can type *set* by itself to get a report of currently defined environment variables.

Examples: The DIRCMD environment variable tells DOS how to display a directory listing; that is, it lets you customize the Directory command so that it automatically includes the switches you prefer to use. For example, to set the normal directory listing so that directories are grouped at the beginning, you could include the following Set command in your AUTOEXEC.BAT file:

```
set dircmd=/o:g
```

An environment variable named TEMP or TMP often appears in AUTOEXEC.BAT files to define a directory that a program can use for storing temporary files as it works. Some programs create their own temporary directories. To define TEMP, first be certain the directory you want to specify already exists or create it with the Make Directory command; for example, type

```
C:\> md c:\temp
```

Then add a line like this to your AUTOEXEC.BAT file:

```
set temp=c:\temp
```

A Sample AUTOEXEC.BAT File

The following lines show a sample AUTOEXEC.BAT file with some typical commands:

```
set comspec=c:\dos\command.com
path c:\dos;c:\windows;c:\word
prompt $p$g
ver
set temp=c:\windows\temp
set dircmd=/w /o:g
mirror c: /tc
```

CONFIG.SYS

Your CONFIG.SYS file contains the instructions DOS needs to work effectively with your computer and its memory, your devices, and your programs. The commands in CONFIG.SYS relate in one way or another to your hardware. When you add a device to your computer setup or install a new application, there's a good chance that you'll have to update your CONFIG.SYS file—or that the installation software that comes with the device or application will do so for you.

COMMANDS FOR CONFIG.SYS

Of the numerous commands you might include in your
CONFIG.SYS file, several are seldom needed and are
safely ignored in this book. Some commands crop up often,
however. Among these are the Buffers, Files, Device, and
Lastdrive commands, described here. These commands can
appear only in CONFIG.SYS. Like DOS commands, the
configuration commands can use either uppercase or lowercase characters. You cannot, however, type them at the
DOS prompt, as you can do with the commands you put in
AUTOEXEC.BAT. Because DOS checks for CONFIG.SYS
only at startup, you must restart your computer for new
configuration commands to take effect.

Several additional configuration commands related to
managing a computer that has extended memory are described in Chapter 8.

Setting the Number of Buffers

When DOS reads from a disk or prepares to write to a disk,
it moves the information in groups of bytes rather than one
at a time. As it collects this information, DOS stores it temporarily in specially reserved portions of memory called
buffers. Buffers function as way stations for data moving to
and from your computer's disks and its memory.

Instead of using one giant buffer, DOS sets aside a number of smaller ones, each capable of holding about 532
bytes of information. Some programs require you to set or
change the number of buffers DOS uses. To do this, you
use the Buffers command.

Command form:

buffers=*number*

□ *number* is the number of buffers you need. You can
specify 1 through 99 buffers.

If you don't specify a different number, DOS assumes a
certain number of buffers based on the type of system you
use: 15 for computers with 512 KB through 640 KB of
memory; fewer for systems with under 512 KB of RAM. If
your computer is slowed by too many disk reads or writes,

you can increase the number of buffers to speed it up. The more buffers you ask DOS to set aside, however, the less memory is available for your programs.

Example: To specify 30 buffers, put this command in your CONFIG.SYS file:

```
buffers=30
```

Setting the Number of Files

Just as Buffers tells DOS the number of buffers to use, Files determines the number of files DOS can keep open at the same time. You probably won't need this command unless the documentation for one of your applications tells you to check for or change a Files command in your CONFIG.SYS file.

Command form:

files=*number*

☐ *number* is the maximum number of files DOS can have open at one time. You can set the number for any value from 8 through 255. DOS requires a minimum of 8, but 20 is a more typical number.

Example: To set the maximum number of open files to 20, put this command in your CONFIG.SYS file:

```
files=20
```

Identifying Devices

DOS routinely uses a number of devices—without requiring any help from you or CONFIG.SYS. For example, it recognizes your keyboard as an expected part of the computer setup. The same is true of drives A, B, and C. The programs, called device drivers, that control these pieces of equipment are built into DOS. Not all device drivers are built into DOS, however. Some, known as installable device drivers, are stored in files on disk. To use an installable device driver, you must first identify it to DOS with a Device command in your CONFIG.SYS file.

In addition to its built-in device drivers, DOS includes some installable device drivers, among them ANSI.SYS, DISPLAY.SYS, EGA.SYS, and PRINTER.SYS. The DOS 5 Setup program adds Device commands for some of these drivers to your CONFIG.SYS file, but if you want to use one of the others, or if you add a new device to your system, you need a Device command to identify the appropriate device driver. Because a single computer setup can have a number of attached devices, you can wind up with several Device commands in CONFIG.SYS. Remember that if you modify CONFIG.SYS to include a new Device command, the new command does not take effect until you restart your computer.

Command form:

device=*driver* [*options*]

□ *driver* is the drive, path, and file specification that tell DOS where to find the device driver file on disk.

□ *options* includes additional information, if any, required by the device driver. One option is shown in the examples below; others are shown in Chapter 8 for the DOS device drivers named SMARTDRV.SYS and RAMDRIVE.SYS. The documentation for a new device should tell you of any options the device driver requires.

Examples: To identify the DOS device driver named ANSI.SYS (stored in the directory C:\DOS), you would place the following command in your CONFIG.SYS file:

```
device=c:\dos\ansi.sys
```

To identify a mouse driver in the WINDOWS directory and add an option (shown as /y here), you would include the following command in CONFIG.SYS:

```
device=c:\windows\mouse.sys /y
```

Configuring the Number of Disk Drives

As you know, DOS identifies disk drives by letter: A, B, C, and so on. Normally, it recognizes up to five disk drives, A through E. You might find that you need more than five

disk drive letters—for example, if you add a new disk
drive to your computer setup, connect to a network, or
create one or more RAM disks (described in Chapter 8) in
your computer's memory. To tell DOS to recognize more
than five drive letters, you use the Lastdrive command.

Command form:

> lastdrive=*letter*

> ☐ *letter* is the highest drive letter you want DOS to
> recognize. It can be any letter up to and including Z.

Example: To tell DOS to recognize 16 drive letters (A
through P), you would include this command in
CONFIG.SYS:

```
lastdrive=p
```

A Sample CONFIG.SYS File

The following lines show a sample CONFIG.SYS file with
some typical configuration commands. Some of these will
appear in your CONFIG.SYS file if Setup put them there.

```
device=c:\dos\setver.exe
files=40
buffers=30
device=c:\dos\ansi.sys
device=c:\windows\mouse.sys /y
device=c:\dos\ega.sys
shell=c:\dos\command.com c:\dos\  /p
lastdrive=p
```

CHAPTER 8

DOS 5 and Memory

Version 5 of DOS marks a significant change from earlier versions, not so much in the way you use DOS as in the way it works with your computer. Before version 5, DOS was able to call on up to 1 MB of memory, using a maximum of 640 KB for programs (including DOS itself) and data. Certain commands could use memory beyond 1 MB, but by and large, DOS could not pass that line, nor could it use more than 640 KB for your work. Version 5 helps DOS contend with the 640-KB/1-MB boundary, enabling DOS to work more efficiently on computers with memory capacities of 1 MB, 2 MB, and more.

This chapter tells you how to check your computer's memory, configure DOS to use high memory, and manage the memory in your computer effectively. It covers the following memory-related DOS 5 features:

■ Memory, for finding out about your computer's memory

■ HIMEM.SYS and EMM386.EXE, for identifying high memory to DOS

■ Dos, for telling DOS to relocate to high memory (and leave the bottom 640 KB for your applications)

■ Devicehigh, for loading device drivers into memory above 640 KB

■ Loadhigh, for loading certain programs into memory above 640 KB

■ SMARTDRV.SYS and RAMDRIVE.SYS, for taking advantage of memory above 1 MB

TYPES OF MEMORY

Computer memory goes by several different names, depending on its type and the way it is used. Although you don't have to worry about what type of memory your computer is using at any given time, you should be able to distinguish among the different types if you have a computer with 1 MB or more of memory. This knowledge is useful not only with DOS but with other programs as well.

Conventional and Upper Memory

DOS has always been able to access 1 MB of memory. This memory is divided into two parts, one of 640 KB and the other of 384 KB. Both are shown in the memory diagram in Figure 8-1. The first 640 KB is the part commonly known as *conventional* memory. DOS and all DOS-based programs use this region of memory without difficulty. You'll sometimes see this called *low* memory.

The 384-KB memory area that sits above the first 640 KB is the *upper* memory area, often called reserved memory. The upper memory area is set aside for video and other special needs. These uses generally don't require all the upper memory area, however, so on certain computers you can use the DOS commands Devicehigh and Loadhigh to

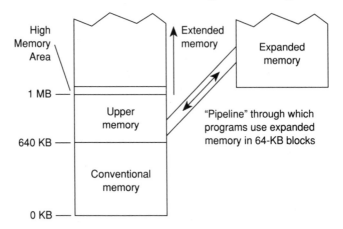

FIGURE 8-1. *DOS manages a variety of memory types.*

load device drivers and certain programs into unused portions of the reserved memory area. This is a new capability with DOS 5, and one of the ways in which DOS 5 makes the best possible use of available memory.

Extended and Expanded Memory

Beyond the basic 1 MB that DOS can reach directly, you can add either or both of two additional types of memory, *extended* and *expanded*. These types of memory are used in very different ways, and you should know roughly what they are because some DOS commands and some programs, such as Windows, can be customized to use one or the other type:

■ Extended memory begins at 1 MB and goes up more or less stacked on top of the upper memory area. The first 64 KB of extended memory is a special portion, known as the High Memory Area, or HMA. Although memory is not a typical device, such as a disk drive, DOS includes a device driver called HIMEM.SYS that manages extended memory.

■ Expanded memory is a separate pool of memory that is, in a sense, set off to the side and available for programs to draw on as needed. The standard for exploiting expanded memory is the Lotus-Intel-Microsoft Expanded Memory Specification, or LIM EMS. To take advantage of expanded memory, programs must be designed to use it, and the memory itself must always be managed by a program called an expanded memory manager.

Imagine the various types of memory as pages in two separate binders. One binder contains 640 pages, a divider, another 384 pages, and a final divider followed by an extra 1000 pages or more. This binder is comparable to your computer's lower 640 KB of conventional memory, the 384 KB of its upper memory area, and any extended memory above 1 MB. The second binder, which is comparable to expanded memory, contains sets of pages, 64 to a set. To use this memory, an expanded memory manager does the equivalent of swapping 64-page sets into the main binder.

MEMORY-MANAGEMENT COMMANDS

The memory-management features of DOS 5 work in concert and are designed for use on computers with an 80286 microprocessor or better and at least 1 MB of memory. To use some of the most advantageous memory-management features of DOS 5, your computer must have an 80386 microprocessor or better.

Checking Your Computer's Memory

When you use DOS commands to manipulate your computer's memory, it's helpful, and sometimes necessary, to know how that memory is being used and how much is available for you to work with. To find out about the memory in your computer, use the Memory command, abbreviated Mem. This information lets you find out how much memory is available for loading device drivers and programs and how much is available for use by applications.

Command form:

mem /c

☐ /c (for classify) produces a report that tells you the names and sizes of programs in memory and how much memory remains free for use.

The Memory command includes two additional switches, /p and /d, that offer very detailed information about your computer's use of memory. You're unlikely to need these switches if you're not a programmer.

If you type the Memory command by itself, *mem*, you see a summary report on your computer's memory, including conventional, extended, and expanded memory and the amount currently available for loading programs.

Examples: To request a report on your computer's memory, type the Memory command without any switches:

```
C:\> mem
```

For a computer with an 80386 microprocessor and 5 MB of extended memory, DOS produces a report like this:

```
655360 bytes total conventional memory
655360 bytes available to MS-DOS
622736 largest executable program size

4194304 bytes total contiguous extended memory
     0 bytes available contiguous extended memory
4172800 bytes available XMS memory
        MS-DOS resident in High Memory Area
```

The first three lines of this report tell you about your computer's conventional memory: how much you have, how much is available to DOS, and how much of the available memory can be used to load a program.

The second part of this report tells you about the extended memory in your computer. (The message *0 bytes available contiguous extended memory* means that all extended memory is accounted for by DOS.) The line *MS-DOS resident in High Memory Area* means that DOS has located itself outside the lower 640 KB of conventional memory it would normally use. This message is one of the most remarkable that DOS 5 displays because it means that DOS has moved part of itself to your computer's extended memory and is leaving as much conventional memory as possible for your applications to use. (Applications are, almost by definition, memory-hungry beasts.)

To see how programs are loaded into your computer's memory, type

```
C:\> mem /c
```

This time, DOS displays a far more detailed report, like the one at the top of the next page.

This report tells you not only which programs are in memory, but also how large they are. The decimal values give program sizes in figures that are easy to understand. The hexadecimal values (the second set of values) give the same sizes in the form you sometimes need for specifying program sizes to DOS — when you use the Devicehigh command, for example. Unless you really want to fine-tune your system, you needn't worry much about program sizes, except to note how much upper memory (listed as UMBs, for upper memory blocks) is available. Knowing how much upper memory is available can help you decide whether you can use the Devicehigh or Loadhigh command, described later, to load another device driver or program into the upper memory area.

```
Conventional Memory :

Name                Size in Decimal        Size in Hex
------------        --------------         -----------
MSDOS               14736    ( 14.4K)      3990
HIMEM               1184     (  1.2K)      4A0
EMM386              8400     (  8.2K)      20D0
COMMAND             3136     (  3.1K)      C40
FREE                64       (  0.1K)      40
FREE                224      (  0.2K)      E0
FREE                627392   (612.7K)      992C0

Total  FREE :       627680   (613.0K)

Upper Memory :

Name                Size in Decimal        Size in Hex
------------        --------------         -----------
SYSTEM              196640   (192.0K)      30020
DOSKEY              3888     (  3.8K)      F30
MOUSE               14320    ( 14.0K)      37F0
FREE                208      (  0.2K)      D0
FREE                61344    ( 59.9K)      EFA0
FREE                51152    ( 50.0K)      C7D0

Total  FREE :       112704   (110.1K)

Total bytes available to programs (Conventional+Upper) :      740384
Largest executable program size :                            627392
Largest available upper memory block :                        61344

   4194304 bytes total contiguous extended memory
         0 bytes available contiguous extended memory
   4172800 bytes available XMS memory
           MS-DOS resident in High Memory Area
```

The Device Drivers

DOS includes two memory-related device drivers, HIMEM.SYS and EMM386.EXE. You can use HIMEM.SYS on any computer with an 80286 microprocessor or better; EMM386.EXE is limited to use with an 80386 or better microprocessor.

Before installation begins, the DOS 5 Setup program checks your computer's microprocessor and memory to determine how DOS should be installed. If appropriate, Setup adds a Device command to your CONFIG.SYS file for the HIMEM.SYS memory device driver. The memory-related device drivers are described below primarily so that you'll know their meaning if you edit your CONFIG.SYS file. To add these commands to CONFIG.SYS, or to modify existing commands, use the formats shown.

HIMEM.SYS

The HIMEM.SYS device driver manages extended memory on your computer, making it available to programs and guaranteeing that they don't encounter any conflicts by attempting to use the same portion of extended memory. In a sense, HIMEM.SYS is the first link in a chain of commands that enable DOS to use memory above 640 KB. If you have a recent 80286 or better computer with 1 MB or more of memory, your computer probably has some extended memory.

If Setup finds extended memory on your computer, it adds a line to your CONFIG.SYS file that installs HIMEM.SYS. If you see this command in CONFIG.SYS, do not experiment with it carelessly. Because DOS must be able to find and use HIMEM.SYS before it can carry out any other memory-management commands, be sure the command to install HIMEM.SYS appears ahead of any other memory-management commands in CONFIG.SYS.

Command form:

device=c:\dos\himem.sys

The command shown here assumes that DOS is in the directory DOS on drive C. Adjust the path if necessary.

EMM386.EXE

The EMM386.EXE device driver works on computers with extended memory. It has two jobs to do. First, it provides DOS with access to the upper memory area, into which you can load other device drivers and certain terminate-and-stay-resident (TSR) programs. Second, it can simulate expanded memory on a computer with extended memory. You can use this capability if your computer has only extended memory and you want to run programs designed to use expanded, but not extended, memory. Your program documentation should provide this information.

As its name indicates, EMM386.EXE is for computers with 80386 microprocessors or better. If your computer has an 80286 microprocessor, you cannot use this device driver, but the machine might be able to use HIMEM.SYS, or a non-DOS device driver that lets you load device drivers and TSR programs into the upper memory area.

Command form:

device=c:\dos\emm386.exe [*memory*][ram | noems]

☐ *memory* is the amount of extended memory, in kilobytes, you want to set aside for use as simulated expanded memory. Specify *memory* as a number from 16 through 32768. Use this switch if you need expanded memory for your programs.

☐ ram is an option that tells DOS you want expanded memory and you also want access to the upper memory area (the memory region between 640 KB and 1 MB) for moving device drivers and TSR programs out of conventional memory, the highly valuable bottom 640-KB region.

☐ noems (no expanded memory) is an option that tells DOS you don't want or need expanded memory. You cannot use both the noems and ram options. Because expanded memory usually requires some space in the upper memory area, the noems option frees the maximum possible space in the upper memory area for loading device drivers and programs.

DOS won't be able to use EMM386.EXE unless it has already loaded the HIMEM.SYS driver, so be sure the Device commands for these drivers appear in CONFIG.SYS in the order shown in the examples below.

Examples: The following commands, in the order shown, give DOS access to the upper memory area and indicate that the system doesn't use any expanded memory:

```
device=c:\dos\himem.sys
device=c:\dos\emm386.exe noems
```

The following commands set aside 340 KB of extended memory for use as simulated expanded memory and indicate that the system needs both expanded memory and access to the upper memory area:

```
device=c:\dos\himem.sys
device=c:\dos\emm386.exe 340 ram
```

Dos

The Dos command is one of the most elegant and useful features of DOS 5 on a computer with even a small amount of extended memory. It frees as much as possible of your computer's low memory (the first 640 KB) by moving much of DOS to the beginning of extended memory, in the High Memory Area.

On a computer equipped with an 80286 microprocessor and extended memory, the Dos command works with HIMEM.SYS to move DOS into the HMA. On a computer with an 80386 or better microprocessor, the Dos command works with both HIMEM.SYS and EMM386.EXE to move DOS into the HMA and to give DOS access to the upper memory area. These two functions, combined with the Devicehigh and Loadhigh commands, can free a substantial amount of conventional memory for your programs and data.

The Dos command works only if it occurs in your CONFIG.SYS file. If the Setup program determines that DOS can be moved into the HMA, it inserts the Dos command in your CONFIG.SYS file.

Command form:

dos=high | low,umb | noumb

- ☐ high and low are either/or options that tell DOS whether to load itself into the High Memory Area. If you specify low or omit the option, DOS loads itself into low memory.

- ☐ umb and noumb are either/or options. They tell DOS whether to maintain an open link to the upper memory area so that device drivers and TSR programs can be loaded into the upper memory area. If you specify noumb or omit the option, DOS doesn't maintain an open link to the upper memory area. You must separate umb or noumb from the high or low option with a comma, as shown in the second example below.

Examples: The following set of commands loads DOS into the high memory area on an 80286 computer with extended memory:

```
device=c:\dos\himem.sys
dos=high
```

This Device command lets DOS use extended memory, and the Dos command loads DOS into high memory.

The following set of commands loads DOS into the High Memory Area and enables it to maintain a link to the upper memory area on an 80386 or better computer with extended memory:

```
device=c:\dos\himem.sys
device=c:\dos\emm386.exe noems
dos=high,umb
```

The first Device command enables DOS to use extended memory. The second enables DOS to use upper memory. Finally, the Dos command loads DOS into the High Memory Area and maintains a link to upper memory.

Devicehigh

After you've laid the groundwork by loading HIMEM.SYS and EMM386.EXE and you've opened a link to the upper memory area with the Dos command, you can add Devicehigh commands to your CONFIG.SYS file or change Device commands to Devicehigh. Either way will enable you to load device drivers into available blocks in the upper memory area. The Devicehigh command requires at least 350 KB of extended memory. If you have enough extended memory, using this command is one way to free additional low memory for applications.

You can use Devicehigh when you install the following DOS device drivers: ANSI.SYS, DISPLAY.SYS, DRIVER.SYS, EGA.SYS, PRINTER.SYS, and RAM-DRIVE.SYS. If Devicehigh cannot find sufficient memory to load a device driver into an upper memory block, it places the device driver in low memory instead.

Notes on using Devicehigh: *If you load a number of device drivers at startup, using Devicehigh in CONFIG.SYS can require some experimenting because different drivers require different amounts of memory. DOS loads device drivers into upper memory one by one, adding as many as it can until it runs out of room. Use the Mem /c command to see how big your device drivers are, to check on which device drivers have been loaded into upper memory, and to see how much room, if any, remains for others. Because some non-DOS device*

*drivers might not load correctly into upper memory and could
cause your computer to experience problems at startup, experiment with your CONFIG.SYS file from a (bootable) floppy
disk rather than from your hard disk.*

Command form:

devicehigh [size=*driversize*] *driver* [*options*]

☐ size=*driversize* is an option you use to specify the
least amount of memory (as a hexadecimal value)
that must be available for DOS to try loading the
device driver into the upper memory area. You
shouldn't need this option, but you can try it if you
encounter problems in loading a specific device
driver into upper memory. To find the value for
driversize, load the device driver into conventional
memory and then use the Mem /c command to check
on its size in hexadecimal.

☐ *driver* is the drive, path, and file specification of the
device driver to load into the upper memory area.

☐ *options* represents any switches or other information
you specify when loading the device driver. For examples of such options, see the sample command
using RAMDRIVE.SYS below.

Examples: The following commands (in your CON-
FIG.SYS file) load the DOS device drivers ANSI.SYS
and EGA.SYS into the upper memory area.

```
device=c:\dos\himem.sys
device=c:\dos\emm386.exe noems
dos=high,umb
devicehigh=c:\dos\ansi.sys
devicehigh=c:\dos\ega.sys
```

The following commands (in your CONFIG.SYS file)
load the device driver RAMDRIVE.SYS into the upper
memory area and create a 1-MB simulated disk drive in
extended memory.

```
device=c:\dos\himem.sys
device=c:\dos\emm386.exe noems
dos=high,umb
devicehigh=c:\dos\ramdrive.sys 1024 /e
```

Loadhigh

Whereas the Devicehigh command loads device drivers
into upper memory, the Loadhigh command—which can
be abbreviated Lh—loads TSR programs into upper
memory. Unlike Devicehigh, Loadhigh works from the
DOS prompt as well as in your CONFIG.SYS file. To load
TSR programs into upper memory each time you start or
restart your computer, place a Loadhigh command for each
of those programs into your AUTOEXEC.BAT file. If DOS
finds insufficient space for loading a program into upper
memory, it loads the program into conventional memory
instead.

Loadhigh works with a number of DOS programs, including Doskey, the DOS Shell, Mode, and Print. To find
out where a program is loaded, use the Mem /c command.

Command form:

lh *program* [*options*]

☐ *program* is the name of the program you want to load
into the upper memory area. Specify the drive and
path, if necessary, in addition to the filename of the
program.

☐ *options* includes any switches or information you
would type when loading the program. (The Print
example below demonstrates the use of an option in a
Loadhigh command.)

Examples: To load the Doskey program into the upper
memory area, either type this command at the DOS
prompt:

```
C:\> lh doskey
```

or place the same command in AUTOEXEC.BAT.

To load the Print program into the upper memory area,
specifying the printer attached to the second parallel
printer port, type the following command (or place it in
AUTOEXEC.BAT):

```
C:\> lh print /d:lpt2
```

Using Extended and Expanded Memory

In addition to loading DOS, device drivers, and TSR programs into parts of memory other than the coveted 640 KB of conventional memory, you can make your computer faster and more efficient by using either extended memory or expanded memory for two special device drivers. The first, SMARTDRV.SYS, creates a disk cache in memory that DOS uses to hold information recently read from disk. If you request that information again, DOS can find it in the disk cache rather than repeating the relatively slow operation of reading the same information from disk. The second device driver, RAMDRIVE.SYS, is just as effective because it, too, bypasses time-consuming trips to disk. RAMDRIVE.SYS sets aside part of your computer's memory as an electronic "disk drive" that DOS uses as if it were a real (physical) disk drive.

SMARTDRV.SYS

To create a disk cache with SMARTDRV.SYS, you add a Device command to CONFIG.SYS. By default, SMARTDRV.SYS uses extended memory for a disk cache. If your computer has both expanded and extended memory, however, you can specify that the cache be in expanded memory, but extended memory is usually more efficient. Once you create a disk cache, DOS manages it for you, so you don't have to worry about filling it, emptying it, or saving anything in it. All that happens automatically.

Caution: On some computers, you can use the Devicehigh command to load SMARTDRV.SYS into the upper memory area. The command can, however, cause problems with startup, so if you want to try this, do so first from a bootable floppy disk.

Command form:

device=c:\dos\smartdrv.sys [*cachesize*] [*minimum*] /a

□ *cachesize* is the size you want the disk cache to be, in kilobytes. DOS creates a disk cache of 256 KB by default, but if you want one smaller or larger, you can specify *cachesize* as any value from 128 through 8192 (128 KB through 8 MB). If DOS cannot find enough memory for the size you specify, it adjusts the size of the disk cache downward to fit.

☐ *minimum* is the minimum size the disk cache can be. You don't have to specify a minimum size, but try specifying *minimum* as 0 if you encounter problems starting Windows 3.0 correctly or if your Windows applications keep running out of memory.

☐ /a tells SMARTDRV.SYS to create the disk cache in expanded memory.

Examples: To create a 1024-KB disk cache in extended memory, you need the following commands in CONFIG.SYS:

```
device=c:\dos\himem.sys
device=c:\dos\smartdrv.sys 1024
```

To create the same-size disk cache in actual expanded memory (not simulated expanded memory), you need these commands in CONFIG.SYS:

```
device=c:\dos\himem.sys
device=c:\dos\emm386.exe
device=c:\dos\smartdrv.sys 1024 /a
```

RAMDRIVE.SYS

The RAMDRIVE.SYS device driver creates a memory-based "disk drive"—a RAM disk—that works like a real disk drive in that you refer to it by drive letter and use it as if it were a real disk drive. You can copy files to it, delete files from it, and request directory listings of files on it. A RAM disk has one great advantage over a real disk drive: It is very fast. It also has one great disadvantage compared to a real disk drive: It exists only in memory, so everything on it disappears when you turn off or restart your computer.

A RAM disk can be a great time-saver when you're working with large programs or files because DOS can access them as quickly as it can access anything else in memory. You must always remember, however, to copy every scrap of information you want to keep onto a real disk before shutting down your computer. If you don't, you lose all your work and cannot get it back. To protect yourself even while you're using a RAM disk, form the habit of saving your work periodically on a real disk.

You create a RAM disk with either the Device or the Devicehigh command, and you can create the disk in conventional, extended, or expanded memory. If you use Devicehigh, the device driver that creates the RAM disk loads into upper memory block; the RAM disk itself is created using whatever type of memory you specify. If you have a choice, create the RAM disk in either extended or expanded memory to avoid using any of the 640 KB of conventional memory you need for other programs.

You can create as many RAM disks as you have available memory. If you need more drive letters, remember to use the Lastdrive command.

Command form:

   device=c:\dos\ramdrive.sys [*disksize*] /e /a

Or:

   devicehigh=c:\dos\ramdrive.sys [*disksize*] /e /a

   □ Device and Devicehigh tell DOS where to load the RAMDRIVE.SYS device driver.

   □ *disksize* specifies the size of the RAM disk, in kilobytes. DOS creates a RAM disk of 64 KB by default, but you can specify any value from a minimum of 16 through a maximum of 16384 (equal to 16 MB).

   □ /e tells DOS to create the RAM disk in extended memory.

   □ /a tells DOS to create the RAM disk in expanded memory.

Examples: To create a RAM disk of 1024 KB in extended memory, you would need to place these commands in CONFIG.SYS:

```
device=c:\dos\himem.sys
device=c:\dos\ramdrive.sys 1024 /e
```

To load the device driver into the upper memory area and create a 1024-KB RAM disk in extended memory, you would need these commands in CONFIG.SYS:

```
device=c:\dos\himem.sys
device=c:\dos\emm386.exe noems
dos=high,umb
devicehigh=c:\dos\ramdrive.sys 1024 /e
```

CHAPTER 9

The DOS Shell

The DOS Shell is a work environment developed by Microsoft and supplied as a part of DOS by many hardware manufacturers. The Shell helps make your work with DOS easier and more visual by creating an on-screen *window* in which it displays files, directories, and sets of menus. Instead of offering a blank screen and expecting you to remember which commands you can use in a given situation, the Shell displays an organized screenful of information related to your disks, files, and programs. With a few keystrokes or a click or two of the mouse, you can choose common commands and options you would otherwise type at the DOS command line.

Designed to be highly interactive and easy to use, the Shell makes working with DOS and your programs less dependent on typed commands and on your own sometimes fallible memory. Although the DOS prompt gives you access to more—and more sophisticated—DOS commands, the Shell offers ease of use, on-screen friendliness, and the ability to perform most of your day-to-day work with DOS.

Even though the Shell is a part of DOS, its visual nature makes using it considerably different from typing equivalent commands at the DOS prompt. Using DOS at the prompt is like walking into a showroom to ask for a brown sedan with a tan interior. Using the Shell is more like choosing a car from a lot full of different models and colors. In one situation, you decide what you want and then ask for it; in the other, you wander around and look for yourself. Some people prefer the first approach, others prefer the second, and still others combine the two. If you're at home with the keyboard and with DOS, you might prefer the speed and efficiency of working at the DOS prompt. If you're a highly visual person, or if you don't expect to use many DOS commands, you might prefer the Shell to the DOS prompt. If you're comfortable with both work-styles, you might find that the Shell is unbeatable in some situations but less effective than DOS in others.

About this chapter: Although the Shell is easy to use, this brief chapter won't give you an in-depth look at its features. The first part of this chapter introduces a special feature of the Shell called online Help. The remainder of the chapter shows you around the Shell and provides you with the tools you need to explore further on your own—probably more fun than reading about the Shell in a book.

STARTING AND STOPPING THE SHELL

If DOS was installed so that the Shell starts whenever you start your computer, all you do is turn on or restart the computer to call up the Shell. If you chose not to run the Shell at startup, you can start it from the DOS prompt whenever you want by typing

`C:\> dosshell`

During startup, the Shell reads directory and file information from the current disk into memory and displays a box that lets you know what's happening. After the information is in memory, the box disappears.

Once you start the Shell, you can work with it as long as you want. You can even switch to DOS without stopping the Shell by pressing Shift-F9; return to the Shell by typing *exit* at the DOS prompt.

When you've finished using the Shell and want to quit, the easiest way is to press the F3 key. If you prefer, you can use the Exit command on the File menu instead.

THE MAIN WINDOW

Until you change its settings, the Shell starts by displaying a large window divided horizontally, as shown in Figure 9-1. The top half shows you the File List, and the lower half shows the Program List. The File List displays a directory tree at the left side of the screen and a list of files in the current directory at the right. The Program List shows the names of programs you can run from the Shell. Each of these lists is described in more detail later.

Parts of the Window

Whenever you use the Shell, it frames its display in a full-screen area, its main window. Within the main window, the Shell often displays smaller windows. Because the Shell is so interactive, a window contains a number of parts that respond to keyboard and mouse actions. These parts are labeled in Figure 9-1.

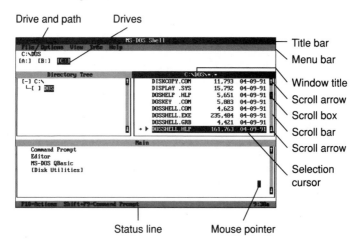

FIGURE 9-1. *The main window of the DOS Shell.*

- Title bar: Identifies the MS-DOS Shell

- Menu bar: Displays the names of menus, which contain commands to choose from

- Drive and path: Displays the current drive and directory

- Drives: Displays the letters of the drives on your computer, including RAM disks; indicates the current drive with a dark highlight

- Scroll bar, scroll arrow, and scroll box: Respond to mouse actions to scroll through a list that cannot be fully displayed in the window

- Window title: Identifies the contents of a window

- Selection cursor: Highlights the current choice in the menu bar, in a directory, or in another list

- Status line: Displays the time and reminds you of two special keystrokes, F10 to activate the menu bar and Shift-F9 to leave the Shell temporarily and work at the DOS prompt

Display Modes

The Shell operates in either of two display modes, *text* or *graphic*. When you first use the Shell, it always appears in text mode: It draws the window with standard screen characters, such as highlighted (bright) letters, square brackets ([ ]), and straight lines. The main window shown in Figure 9-1 is displayed in text mode.

In graphics mode, the Shell becomes a bit more flamboyant, making use of small graphical elements (*icons*) that let you identify items at a glance.

If you choose, and if your computer's display hardware can work with it, you can change the Shell to graphics mode, in which the main window looks like this:

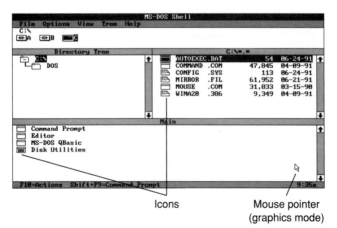

Icons   Mouse pointer
(graphics mode)

The display mode you use doesn't affect the way you work with the Shell. You might find text mode slightly faster because your computer can more easily update the display, but aside from this nominal consideration, the choice between text and graphics modes is up to you.

If you want to experiment with display modes, read the following sections on using menus and then try the Display command on the Options menu. The choices offered by this command match the capabilities of your hardware, so you can choose and preview any display modes in the list.

Selecting Items

The Shell uses your computer's screen to display basic information about your disks and files, so your work with the Shell primarily involves selecting items and then choosing commands to act upon those items. You can use either the keyboard or the mouse with the Shell. If you're accustomed to a mouse, you'll probably find it a faster and more efficient way to use the Shell than clattering away at the keyboard. You perform the same types of mouse actions in the Shell as you do in other graphical programs:

■ Click (press and release the left button once) to open a menu, choose a command, or select an item in a window.

■ Double-click (press and release the left button twice in quick succession) to carry out a command, go to a topic in a Help window, or run a program.

■ Drag (press the left button and hold it down while moving the mouse) to move a file.

As a general rule, when you use the keyboard:

■ Press the Tab key to move from one part of the Shell window to another and to move among choices in a window or dialog box. Hold down Shift and press the Tab key (Shift-Tab) to move in the opposite direction.

■ Press the direction keys to move the selection cursor up or down in a menu or a list.

■ Press the Enter key to carry out a selected command.

■ Press either F10 or the Alt key to activate the menu bar.

■ Press the highlighted (in text mode) or underlined (in graphics mode) letter in a menu name to open the menu; press the highlighted or underlined letter in a command name to choose the command.

Sometimes these basic mouse and keyboard actions are combined with certain special keys. These combinations are noted at the appropriate points in the chapter. They are also listed in the online Help for the Shell, described next.

HELP

After you're familiar with basic Shell features, the Shell's online Help can give you all the details you need to use the Shell. You can request help in either of two ways: by opening the Help menu in the menu bar or by pressing the F1 key after you've chosen a command or command option. Using the Help menu is a good way to learn about the Shell and to discover what it can do. Pressing F1 takes you directly to information about the command or option you chose before requesting help. The two Help techniques can assist you with any Shell procedure you undertake.

Using the Help Menu

To use the Help menu (or any other Shell menu), click the mouse on the name of the menu you want, or press either F10 or the Alt key:

■ If you use the mouse, clicking on a menu name or a command name chooses the item, so clicking on Help immediately opens the Help menu.

■ If you use the keyboard, the selection cursor (a dark box) appears in the menu bar, and the first letter of each menu name changes to a highlighted or an underlined character. The highlighting or underline in a menu name or a command name means that you can press that letter to choose the item. To choose the Help menu, press H. As soon as you do, the menu opens.

Whichever method you use, you see the menu below.
Like other menus, it offers a list of choices related to the
menu name.

On the Help menu, you can choose to see an outlined list of
Help topics (*Index*), help on using the keyboard with the
Shell (*Keyboard*), information about the Shell (*Shell Basics*),
details on Shell commands (*Commands*), information on
ways to perform different tasks (*Procedures*), help with
using Help (*Using Help*), or some copyright information
(*About Help*).

To choose a particular topic, you do one of the
following:

■ Click on the topic with the mouse.

■ Use the Up and Down direction keys, if necessary, to
move the selection cursor to the topic you want, and
then press Enter.

■ Press the key that corresponds to the highlighted or underlined character in the topic name.

Choosing a topic opens a Help window in the middle of
the screen, with information related to the topic you chose.
For example, if you choose Index, you see a window like
the one below:

```
                       MS-DOS Shell Help
                    MS-DOS Shell Help Index
 To see a topic:                                               ↑

  - Double-click the topic.

 Or                                          _-- -

  - Press TAB to select the topic you want, and then press ENTER.

 KEYBOARD HELP

 →   General MS-DOS Shell Keys                                  ↓


      Close        Back        Keys        Index        Help
```

The index, like the index of a book, lists the various categories of Help you can choose to look at. The first part of the display tells you how to choose a topic. To scroll through the index, use your mouse and the scroll bar along the right edge of the Help window, or press the PgDn and PgUp keys to move one screen at a time and the Up and Down direction keys to move one line at a time.

Unlike the entries in a book index, the items in the Help index are not arranged alphabetically. Scrolling through the index, you'll find a series of major topics that essentially match the other items on the Help menu: keyboard, commands, procedures, Shell basics, and help on using Help. Under these topics are the entries, highlighted or displayed in a different color. You can use either the mouse or the keyboard to choose the entry that interests you.

- With the mouse, double-click on the entry.

- With the keyboard, press the Tab key until the selection cursor highlights the entry, and then press Enter.

When you choose an entry, the window contents change to display information on the subject you chose. As you use Help, you will notice that the subjects you choose end with a list of related entries. Using the same method outlined above, you can move from topic to topic, subject to subject, following Help until you find the information you need or until you exhaust the subject.

Help Buttons

As you move through Help, you see a set of buttons at the bottom of the Help window:

- Close: Closes the Help window (this is the same as pressing the Esc key)

- Back: Moves back to the previous topic

- Keys: Goes to Help on using the keyboard to maneuver in the Shell

- Index: Displays the Help index

- Help: Explains how to use Help

To choose one of these buttons with the mouse, click on the appropriate button. To choose a button with the keyboard, press the Tab key until the cursor (a small underline) appears in the button, and then press Enter.

USING MENUS

The Shell's menus offer lists of commands or options you can choose. There are five basic menus: File, Options, View, Tree, and Help. Although you might not be aware of it at first, the menus aren't always the same and don't always offer the same choices. What you can do in a given situation depends on what item or items you've selected in the Shell window. The distinction makes plenty of sense when you think about it, because there are certain operations you can perform on files and others you can perform with programs. The Shell is "smart" enough to offer you the appropriate choices. The following illustration shows a typical menu with descriptions of notable features in it:

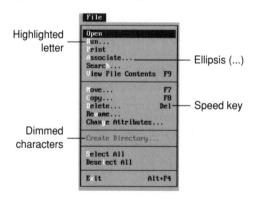

To choose a command or an option from a menu, perform one of the following actions: Click on the item with your mouse, press the key that corresponds to the highlighted or underlined letter in the item name, or highlight the item and press Enter. A few menu choices are "toggle" items that you turn on and off depending on how you want the Shell to behave. These choices appear in the Options menu and are described in the menu section at the end of this chapter. To turn these items on or off, simply choose them from the menu.

Using Dialog Boxes

If an ellipsis (...) appears as part of a menu item, as in *Search*..., the symbol means that the Shell will need additional information to complete that command. If you choose the command, the Shell will display a *dialog box* requesting more detail. A dialog box is the Shell's way of presenting you with equivalents of the command options and switches you type at the DOS prompt. Dialog boxes use four methods of requesting information, each of which is explained below.

■ *Text boxes* are rectangular boxes in which you type file specifications and other such information. Sometimes the Shell displays a suggested response (such as *.*) in a text box; at other times, it simply displays empty text boxes for you to fill. To enter text, tab to the text box if necessary. When the highlight is in the box, start typing to "fill in the blank" or to replace a suggested response. If you want to modify the suggested response, click with the mouse or use the direction keys to position the cursor in the displayed text and insert new characters.

■ *List boxes* are rectangular boxes that contain lists of related items you can choose. To choose an item in a list box, click on it with the mouse, or tab to the list and press the direction keys to highlight the item you want. To move more quickly through a long list box, you can press the first letter in the name of an item to move the highlight to the first item beginning with that letter.

■ *Check boxes* are indicated by square brackets [ ] next to an item you can turn on or off. If the item is turned on, an X appears inside the brackets. To turn an item on or off, click on it with the mouse, or tab to it and press the Spacebar.

■ *Option buttons* appear next to lists of options that, again, represent items you can turn on or off. Option buttons are displayed as circles in graphics mode and sets of parentheses ( ) in text mode. To turn on an option, click on it with the mouse, or tab to the list and press the Up or Down direction key to choose the option you want.

Text box with suggested response

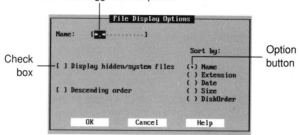

Check box

Option button

FIGURE 9-2. *The File Display Options dialog box demonstrates three methods of obtaining information.*

To see an example of a text box, check boxes, and option buttons, see Figure 9-2 above (the File Display Options dialog box on the Options menu); to see a list box, choose the Display command on the Options menu.

The bottom of a dialog box includes several command buttons you use to carry out the command, request Help, cancel the command, and so on. To use the command buttons, click the mouse on the one you want or tab to the button and press Enter to choose it. If, at any time, you run into trouble using a dialog box, press F1 for Help.

THE FILE LIST AND PROGRAM LIST

When you start the Shell for the first time, you see the main window, illustrated earlier in Figure 9-1. The top half of this window represents the Shell's File List, shown in Figure 9-3 on the next page. The File List shows the directory listing for the current drive and the list of files in the current directory. The Program List, in the bottom half of the window, displays the names of programs you can run from the Shell. You can change the main window with commands on the View menu, but for ease of reference, the following descriptions refer to this basic Shell window.

The File List

Although it displays a directory tree, highlights the current directory, and lists the files in that directory, the File List

```
                              MS-DOS Shell
 File  Options  View  Tree  Help
  C:\DOS
  [A:]  [B:]  [C:]

     Directory Tree                          C:\DOS\*.*
  [-] C:\                        │     DISKCOPY.COM      11,793  04-09-91
    └─[ ] DOS                    │     DISPLAY .SYS      15,792  04-09-91
                                 │     DOSHELP .HLP       5,651  04-09-91
                                 │     DOSKEY  .COM       5,883  04-09-91
                                 │     DOSSHELL.COM       4,623  04-09-91
                                 │     DOSSHELL.EXE     235,484  04-09-91
                                 │     DOSSHELL.GRB       4,421  04-09-91
                                 │  → ▶ DOSSHELL.HLP     161,763  04-09-91
```

FIGURE 9-3. *The File List occupies the top half of the main window.*

is more than just an information window. You can use it to
view different directories and to select files for copying,
deleting, and other file-related operations.

The Directory Tree

The left side of the File List area normally shows the directory tree of the current disk. The directory tree always
begins with the root directory at the top, and with other
directory levels laid out below. The current directory is
highlighted by the selection cursor, and the files in it appear in the list of filenames to the right of the tree, as
shown in Figure 9-3.

To select a different drive, either click on the desired
drive icon with the mouse, or tab the selection cursor to the
drive icons, use the Left or Right direction key to highlight
the desired drive, and then press Enter.

To select a different directory, click on the directory
name, or tab the selection cursor to the directory tree (if
necessary) and then move the selection cursor with the direction keys. If the directory tree is long, you can move up
or down in the tree by using the scroll bar with the mouse
or by pressing the PgUp and PgDn keys on the keyboard.
As you select different directory names, you'll notice that
the list of filenames to the right changes so that it always
reflects the contents of the currently highlighted directory.

The directory tree itself looks much like the output of
the DOS Tree command: level beneath level, with lines and
indents showing the relationships among the directories. To
see different levels of detail on your directory tree, move
the selection cursor to the desired directory and use the
commands on the Tree menu.

The List of Filenames

The list of filenames to the right of the directory tree shows all files in the currently selected directory, as shown in Figure 9-3.

When you want to use a file-related command such as Copy or Delete, you can select one file, several consecutive files, several nonconsecutive files, or all files in the directory (a quick way to select files when you want to move or delete them so you can remove the directory). These are the ways you can select files:

- To select a single file: With the mouse, click on the desired filename. With the keyboard, press Tab to move the selection cursor to the filenames portion of the window; use the PgUp or PgDn or the Up and Down direction keys to move the selection cursor to the filename.

- To select a set of files that appear one after the other in the list: With the mouse, click on the first filename in the set, hold down the Shift key, and click on the last filename in the set. With the keyboard, move the selection cursor to the first filename, hold down the Shift key, and press the Down direction key until the highlight extends to cover the last filename in the set.

- To select a set of files that don't appear sequentially in the list: With the mouse, click on each filename, holding down the Ctrl key until you've selected the last one. With the keyboard, press Shift-F8 and use the direction keys to move from one filename to the next; press the Spacebar to select each filename; press Shift-F8 again to turn off the extended-selection mode, identified by the word *ADD* at the right edge of the status line. (If you mistakenly press Shift-F9, the Shell disappears and you see the DOS prompt. To return to the Shell, type *exit*.)

The Program List

In the Program List area at the bottom of the window, the Shell displays programs and groups of programs you can run. Normally, you see a single region like the one on the following page.

Individual program

```
                                      Main
  ┌─ Command Prompt                                                    ↑
  │  Editor
  │  MS-DOS QBasic
  ▓  Disk Utilities


                                                                       ↓
 F10=Actions  Shift+F9=Command Prompt                          9:53a
```

Program group

Individual programs are associated with a plain, boxlike icon in graphics mode, as shown here. In text mode, such program items are plain and unadorned. Groups of programs, which can include several individual but related programs, are associated with a more elaborate icon in graphics mode and, in text mode, are enclosed in square brackets, like this: *[Disk Utilities]*.

Program Items and Program Groups

Just as a directory can contain both individual files and directories, the Program List can contain both individual programs (*program items*) and groups of related programs (*program groups*). Until you add programs and groups of your own, the Program List offers three program items you can run—Command Prompt, Editor, and MS-DOS QBasic (a programming language)—and one program group, Disk Utilities. All program items represent DOS commands you can run from the Shell.

Running a Program Item

When you choose a program item from the Program List, the Shell starts the program for you. If you choose Command Prompt, the "program" is DOS, and starting the program takes you to the DOS prompt. If you choose Editor, the program is the MS-DOS Editor. When you quit a program, you return to the Shell.

You choose and start a program in much the same way you select files and directories in the File List:

■ With the mouse, double-click on the program name.

■ With the keyboard, tab to the Program List, move the selection cursor to the program name, and press Enter.

If you choose to run Command Prompt from the Shell, your disk drive becomes active for a short time, and then you see the familiar

C:\>

At this point, you can type and carry out any DOS command you want. When you finish, you "quit" DOS by typing *exit* at the DOS prompt. Whenever you use DOS from the Shell, this is your "return to the Shell" command. With a program like the Editor or (if you add it to the Shell) your word processor, you use whatever quit command you would normally use.

Choosing a Program from a Group

If you choose to run a program that belongs to a program group, you add one step to the process: First you open the group to see what program items it contains, and then you choose the program you want to run. Beyond that, running programs from a group is identical to running individual programs in the Program List. For example, the program group Disk Utilities includes a number of DOS commands. To open the group, do one of the following:

■ Double-click with your mouse on *Disk Utilities*

■ Move the selection cursor to *Disk Utilities* and press Enter

Whichever method you choose, the Program List changes to show you the list of program items in the Disk Utilities group:

■ Main, which takes you back to the original Program List

■ Disk Copy, Backup Fixed Disk, Restore Fixed Disk, Quick Format, Format, and Undelete—all of which represent DOS commands you can use from the Shell

To return to Main, you would double-click on *Main*, or highlight it and press Enter. To choose a program item, such as Format, you would double-click on it, or highlight it and press Enter. If, for example, you choose Format, a dialog box appears. Use the dialog box to specify the disk to format (and other options, such as disk size). When you carry out the command, the Shell takes you to DOS, which

formats the disk and then returns you to the Shell. When
you're using the Shell, running programs from the Program
List in this way is much easier than quitting, returning to
the DOS prompt, running the program, and then restarting
the Shell.

Adding Programs to the Program List

You can add any programs you want to the Program List—
your word processor, spreadsheet program, checkbook
balancer, games, or whatever. Keep the list within reason,
however. Stand-alone programs are fine, but a second
operating environment, such as Windows, or a Windows-
based program would not be a good choice because you
would be taxing DOS and your computer's memory. You
would also be duplicating functionality—loading two or
more software levels that offer essentially the same capabilities. Doing this can cause problems, especially if you
try to run multiple programs at the same time by using the
Shell's Task Swapper.

To add a program to the Program List, first move the
selection cursor to the Program List, and then open the File
menu—it changes dramatically when you move between
the File List and the Program List. When you are working
in the File List, the File menu enables you to copy, move,
delete, and otherwise manage your files and directories.
When you are working in the Program List, the same menu
provides options that, among other things, help you add a
program or a program group (*New*), run a program (*Run*),
and define a program (*Properties*).

By way of example, the following procedure shows, in
abbreviated form, how you would add an item called *Disk
Safety*, which runs the DOS Mirror command from the Program List.

To Add a Program Item: Begin by choosing New from the
File menu. The Shell displays a dialog box with option buttons indicating you can choose either a new Program Group
or a new Program Item. The latter is already checked, so
you can choose it by clicking on the OK button or by pressing Enter.

After you choose to add a program item, the screen changes to show another dialog box, this one titled Add Program. In it are blank text boxes in which you can type a title, the command(s) that start the program, a startup directory (if needed), and a shortcut key (if you want one). To add Disk Safety to the Program List, type *Disk Safety* in the Program Title area, press Tab, and then type *mirror %1* in the Commands area, as shown below. The title will appear in the Program List as the name of the program.

```
┌─────────────────────Add Program─────────────────────┐
│                                                      │
│ Program Title . . . . [Disk Safety·················]  │
│                                                      │
│ Commands  . . . . . . [mirror %1··················]  │
│                                                      │
│ Startup Directory . . [·························]     │
│                                                      │
│ Application Shortcut Key     [··················]     │
│                                                      │
│ [X] Pause after exit      Password . .  [·········]  │
│                                                      │
│    ┌──────┐   ┌────────┐   ┌──────┐   ┌──────────┐   │
│    │  OK  │   │ Cancel │   │ Help │   │ Advanced...│  │
│    └──────┘   └────────┘   └──────┘   └──────────┘   │
└──────────────────────────────────────────────────────┘
```

%1 and What It Means: When you're adding a program item to the Program List, you sometimes want to be able to customize the way the program runs—in this case, you want to be able to specify which disk the Mirror command will affect. Including a percent symbol, plus a number from 1 through 9, as part of the command causes the Shell (and DOS) to substitute the items you type after the command name for %1, %2, and so on. By specifying the command as *mirror %1*, you're including a symbol that allows you to specify a disk drive when you run your program: for example, *mirror a:*, *mirror c:*, or *mirror d:*. The Shell substitutes the *a:*, *c:*, or *d:* you type for the *%1* in your Mirror command.

To Create a Dialog Box: When you press Enter after filling out the Add Program dialog box, yet another dialog box appears—this one because you typed *%1* as part of the command. The Shell asks you to create a dialog box of your own that enables the person using the Disk Safety program item to supply a replacement for %1. By filling in the blanks as shown on the next page,

```
┌─────────────────── Add Program ───────────────────┐
│                                                    │
│  Fill in information for % 1    prompt dialog.     │
│                                                    │
│  Window Title . . . .   [Which drive?··············]│
│                                                    │
│  Program Information .   [Please specify a drive letter····]│
│                                                    │
│  Prompt Message . . .   [Drive··············]      │
│                                                    │
│    Default Parameters . .   [C:··············]     │
│                                                    │
│       ┌────────┐      ┌────────┐     ┌────────┐    │
│       │   OK   │      │ Cancel │     │  Help  │    │
│       └────────┘      └────────┘     └────────┘    │
└────────────────────────────────────────────────────┘
```

you create the following dialog box:

```
┌─────────────── Which drive? ───────────────┐
│                                             │
│  Please specify a drive letter              │
│                                             │
│  Drive              [C:··················]  │
│  ┌────────┐      ┌────────┐     ┌────────┐  │
│  │   OK   │      │ Cancel │     │  Help  │  │
│  └────────┘      └────────┘     └────────┘  │
└─────────────────────────────────────────────┘
```

Press Enter to create the dialog box; when you're finished, a new item, *Disk Safety*, appears in the Program List. If you choose this item, the Shell displays your dialog box to prompt for a drive letter, proposing *C:* as the default (suggested drive). When it carries out the command, it runs the DOS Mirror command on the specified drive and, when finished, prompts you to press a key to return to the Shell.

You follow the same procedure in creating a program group, except that you start out by choosing Program Group in the New Program Object dialog box. Once the group is created, choose it from the Program List, and then proceed as outlined above to add programs to it.

Running Multiple Programs with the Task Swapper

One of the advantages of running the Shell is its ability to keep more than one program active in memory at the same time and allow you to switch from one to the other without starting one, quitting it, starting another, quitting it, and so on and on. To activate this feature, choose the item Enable Task Swapper from the Options menu. When you do, the Program List area divides down the middle, and a new miniwindow titled Active Task List appears on the right side. When you start programs, their names appear in this list, and you can move from the Shell to a particular program simply by double-clicking on its name with the mouse or by highlighting its name and pressing Enter. To move from a program to the Shell, press Ctrl-Esc. If you have several programs running at the same time:

■ Hold down Alt and press the Tab key repeatedly to cycle through the programs in the list.

■ Press Alt-Esc to switch to the next program in the list.

■ Press Shift-Alt-Esc (all three keys at once) to switch to the previous program in the list.

When you have one or more programs running under the Shell's control, remember that you must close each one of them before you can quit the Shell.

TO START OR NOT TO START

No matter whether you chose to start or not to start the Shell when the DOS Setup program asked for your preference, you're not stuck with your decision. If, after using the Shell, you decide you made the wrong choice, one quick change to your AUTOEXEC.BAT file is all you need.

If you decide you want to start the Shell each time you start your computer, add this line to the end of your AUTOEXEC.BAT file:

```
dosshell
```

If you later decide you don't want to run the Shell at the end of every startup, modify the command in your AUTOEXEC.BAT file by changing it to this:

```
rem dosshell
```

Adding *rem* before the command tells DOS to ignore the command (to treat it as a remark). You could delete the line if you wanted, but unless your AUTOEXEC.BAT file is crammed with unwanted commands, using *rem* works just as well. It also has the advantage of leaving the command in AUTOEXEC.BAT in case you change your mind again (in which case, delete the *rem*).

This concludes a quick and necessarily superficial look at the Shell. There's much more to see, so if you want more details on any feature, command, option, or procedure, remember the Shell's Help.

Afterword

Moving On

The nine chapters of this reference have provided basic information about your computer and its operating system. Although there is much more to DOS, you have what you need to work productively with your disks, files, and hardware. As your experience grows, you will develop more of your own habits and preferences, and you will want to explore advanced techniques for adapting DOS to your needs.

You can use Doskey to create keyboard macros—long sequences of keystrokes that you can replay by typing a short macro name. And if you're like most experienced DOS users, you'll also want to create your own batch files—sets of DOS commands that you save with the extentension BAT and run as a group by typing the name of the file.

Other References from Microsoft Press

Running MS-DOS, 5th edition, by Van Wolverton (DOS basics, including commands, batch files, input/output redirection, and keyboard macros)

Supercharging MS-DOS, 3rd edition, by Van Wolverton and Dan Gookin (advanced DOS topics, including display and printer control, memory management, and batch files)

Microsoft Quick Reference Series: MS-DOS Batch Files, 2nd edition, by Kris Jamsa (batch files and batch-file commands)

Microsoft Quick Reference Series: MS-DOS, 5th edition, by Van Wolverton (guide to MS-DOS commands)

Microsoft Quick Reference Series: Hard Disk Management, 3rd edition, by Van Wolverton (guide to managing a hard disk with DOS commands)

Managing Memory with DOS 5, by Dan Gookin (memory management on computers with DOS 5)

Index

Special Characters

* (asterisk) as wildcard 64–65
+ (plus sign) in combining files 81, 82
. (period) in filenames 62
.. (parent directory) 95, 96
... (ellipsis) 163, 164
/ (slash) 31
: (colon) 30
> (greater-than sign) as redirection operator 100, 116–17
? (question mark) as wildcard 64
\ (backslash) 90, 91, 94, 96
¦ (vertical bar) in More command 77, 123

A

active drive 29
Add Program dialog box 171
allocation units 41, 48, 49
ANSI.SYS device driver 117, 137, 148, 149
applications 19, 112. *See also* program files
archive file attribute 75. *See also* backups
ASCII files. *See* text files
asterisk (*) as wildcard 64–65
Attribute command 75–76
attributes
  assigning to files 75–76
  listing files by 73–74
  removing from files 76
AUTOEXEC.BAT file 26–27, 129
  changing 127–28

AUTOEXEC.BAT file,
  continued
  DOS commands for 130–34
  and extended memory 125
  loading into Editor 126
  pronouncing 124
  safeguarding 57, 125
  sample 134
  setting DOS prompt in 131–33
  setting environment variables in 133–34
  setting search path in 93, 130–31
  starting Shell in 173
  viewing 125
AUX 111. *See also* LPT ports

B

backslash (\) 90, 91, 94, 96
Backspace key 9, 28, 128
Backup command 107–9
  backing up changed files 107, 109
  creating log file 108, 109
  formatting backup disk 108
backups
  importance of 102–3
  using Backup and Restore commands 107–9
Bad command or file name message 28
bad sectors 41
BAS filename extension 66
baud rate 119, 120
binary digits 111
bits 111, 112. *See also* data bits
bits per second (bps) 119
bootable disks 44–45, 57, 125

JoAnne Woodcock

JoAnne Woodcock is currently a master writer/editor for Microsoft Press. She is coauthor of *Microsoft Word Style Sheets*, published by Microsoft Press.

The manuscript for this book was prepared and submitted to Microsoft Press in electronic form. Text files were processed and formatted using Microsoft Word.

Principal word processor: Debbie Kem

Principal proofreader: Shawn Peck

Principal typographer: Carolyn Magruder

Interior text designer: Darcie S. Furlan

Principal illustrator: Lisa Sandburg

Cover designer: Rebecca Johnson

Text composition by Microsoft Press in Times Roman with display type in Futura Heavy, using the Magna composition system and the Linotronic 300 laser imagesetter.

Printed on recycled paper stock.

The Authorized Editions on DOS 5!

RUNNING MS-DOS, 5th ed.
Van Wolverton

*"An eloquent waltz through the treacherous command line....
A lucid explanation of what DOS is and what DOS does."*

PC Magazine

If you want to learn more about MS-DOS, turn to RUNNING MS-DOS, 5th ed., now updated to include DOS 5. This is the ideal book for all levels—from novices to advanced DOS users. For novices, this is a solid introduction to basic DOS concepts and applications. For seasoned users this book provides all you need to achieve DOS mastery—precise, real-world examples, thoughtful discussions, and understandable descriptions. The author addresses the exciting improvements in DOS 5 while providing in-depth coverage of every major version of DOS. You'll discover how to

- increase your productivity with the new DOS shell
- use the new sort and search capabilities of the Directory command
- create keyboard macros and batch files with the Doskey utility
- edit text files with the new menu-based MS-DOS editor

Also included is a completely revised and updated command reference—an invaluable resource for every DOS user. More than two million readers can't be wrong. This is the most popular DOS book available!

592 pages, softcover   7³/₄ x 9¹/₄ $24.95   Order Code RUMS5

SUPERCHARGING MS-DOS, 3rd ed.

Van Wolverton and Dan Gookin

"If you want to learn how to make DOS jump through hoops, this is probably where you want to start." **MicroTimes**

When you're ready for more—turn to SUPERCHARGING MS-DOS. This sequel to *Running MS-DOS* provides tips for intermediate to advanced business users on maximizing the power of DOS. Updated for DOS 5, the authors have packed the book with proven strategies for

- maximizing productivity with DOS
- using DOS with Windows
- using Epson and HP LaserJet printers
- managing memory effectively

You'll also find scores of new batch files and examples to help you get the most out of DOS. Become a power user with this great resource!

425 pages, softcover 7³/₄ x 9¹/₄ $24.95 Order Code SUMS3

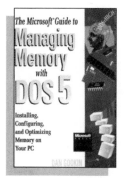

THE MICROSOFT® GUIDE TO MANAGING MEMORY WITH DOS 5

Dan Gookin

"Now you can get your full dollar's worth out of all that memory in your computer."

From the Introduction

One of the most significant features of DOS 5 is its ability to effectively use extended and expanded memory to shatter the 640K barrier. If you're a beginning to intermediate DOS 5 user, this official guide provides clear information on how this is done. Here's what's covered:

- the basics of memory—what it is and how your computer uses it
- the differences between conventional, extended, and expanded memory—in clear English
- buying, installing, and using RAM chips and memory boards
- tips on running the Windows environment more efficiently with DOS 5
- and much more

208 pages, softcover 6 x 9 $14.95 Order Code GUMAME